MW01167569

Best of Success!

Can Any Small Business Make You Rich?

By Michael J. McGroarty

for McGroarty Enterprises Inc.
P.O. Box 338
Perry, Ohio 44081
Phone: 440-259-4306
Fax: 440-259-4306
http://TurntheCrankMarketing.com

authorHOUSE®

AuthorHouse™
1663 Liberty Drive, Suite 200
Bloomington, IN 47403
www.authorhouse.com
Phone: 1-800-839-8640

First published by AuthorHouse 3/24/2008

ISBN: 978-1-4343-7824-8 (sc)
ISBN: 978-1-4343-7823-1 (hc)

Library of Congress Control Number: 2008902455

Printed in the United States of America
Bloomington, Indiana

This book is printed on acid-free paper.

I dedicate this book to my mother.

Mom was smart, talented, and
could do anything she set her mind to,
from making incredibly beautiful crafts, to three
times a week - dressed in a business suit -
removing the valve cover from her tired,
worn out, 1965 Mustang to manually oil the
rocker arms before leaving for work.
(True story.)

But most of all, Mom was loved.

You reap what you sow in this world and
Mom was loved by many. At her funeral
I saw the many faces that she touched in
her life. The people who she loved when
they needed it the most.

Table of Contents

Rich! What is Rich?

Rich is an interesting word. According to every definition that I've read, it means something good. Rich chocolate is good, if you ask me.

Does a lot of money make you rich? In one sense of the word, I suppose it does. But there's more to it than that. When I was in the landscaping business I worked for people who had a lot of money. Most of them did not seem all that happy. Then when I was repairing furnaces, I worked for people who had almost no money at all. Many of them were very poor, but the most honest group of people I've ever dealt with. Most of them seemed content and happy.

In my mind I spent a lot of time trying to balance and compare those two worlds. It was a valuable experience for me and it's reflected in how I handle any amount of money that I have today. I over tip those who work hard for their money, and I make sure I give all I can to my favorite charities.

When I was a kid the family down the road thought we were a rich family because we had a color TV. Even though it was given to us by my great aunt because she and Mom argued over how to change the channels. Next thing I knew, she sent us the TV. Oh well, that was just one of the many eccentric things that Aunt Mona did.

The family down the road was really poor. Their father died when all five children were very young, and their mother worked very hard at low paying jobs just to keep them fed. They had no car and she depended on others to take her places that were too far to walk.

One summer my mom and dad decided to take everyone in their entire family to West Virginia so they could visit relatives. We all went except my sister. Three adults and seven children in my dad's 1962 Chevrolet Impala, screaming for ice cream the entire six hour journey, piled on top of one another.

Looking back on those days - all of us jumping in the back of my dad's old rickety pickup truck for an evening on the shores of Lake Erie, or swimming in the river, endless hours of baseball in the neighbor's front yard, sleeping out in the woods, or the two-week camping trips spent sleeping in tents during torrential downpours - yeah, I think we were all rich. The kind of rich that money can't buy. Never lose sight of that.

But I suspect you bought this book because you are pursuing that other kind of rich. The monetary kind. The kind of rich that seems so easy for some, and completely out of reach to others. What's the secret? How do some people do it so easily, while most of the population lives paycheck to paycheck?

I can not promise you monetary riches. However, you are about to discover a number of very powerful strategies that have propelled others to great success. Apply them to your life and your business and you will see results.

Really successful entrepreneurs do a lot of "little" things differently than most small business owners. These little things are not difficult to do, nor are they complicated or hard to understand. But to most people they go unnoticed.

It's just that most small business owners start their business with the assumption of "if you build it, they will come". That may work with a baseball field on a farm out in the middle of nowhere, although I highly doubt it, but it does not work that way in business. In business you have to work really hard to get customers, keep customers, attract *the right kind of customers* in the first place, and concentrate on the part of your business that is the most profitable.

There are two actions that will bring you the kind of success you are seeking with your small business. Each has several steps. You must figure out exactly what they are, and how to apply them to both your daily life and your business.

1. In order to realize incredible success with a small business, you need to adopt and stringently follow some basic, yet extremely important success principles. The success principles that I am going to spell out for you here work incredibly well. At first they may seem a little too simple to make a difference. But this is what I want you to do. I want you to type them out on a little card,

then put that card in your pocket and refer to it daily.

By doing this you will discover that, up until now, you have not been following these success principles. But if you carry the card to remind yourself of exactly what you need to do each day, you will without a doubt see a huge difference in your success after a month, six months, then a year. If you follow all of the suggestions in this book, you will see an incredible increase in net profit from your small business.

2. The second action that will make you incredibly successful is to develop and implement daily an action plan to grow your business. Later in this book you are going to learn a lot about a system that I call "Turn the Crank Marketing". If you use and implement this "Turn the Crank Marketing" system it can make your small business incredibly successful. "Turn the Crank Marketing" works! Plain and simple, it works. Don't dismiss it as more worthless theory.

Fourteen Success Principles to Write Down and Follow:

1. Review your written goals daily.
2. Use every minute of every day.
3. Stop procrastinating.
4. Force yourself to do the things you don't like to do.
5. Have more entrepreneurial thoughts.
6. Time block.
7. Work on the 80%/20% rule.
8. Advertise aggressively.

9. Stop the time wasters.
10. Think bigger.
11. Join a mastermind group.
12. Deposit into your wealth account.
13. Think accurately.
14. Tap every knowledge base that you can.

This is important. Type that list out on a small pocket-sized card, make several copies, have them laminated, then keep them where you will be forced to review them daily.

Do this simple exercise with the little cards. These fourteen strategies have, and continue to produce profound improvements in my life and my business.

Review Your Written Goals Daily

I read something on business, success, marketing, or making money every day and have been doing so for well over twenty years. I think every single publication that I've read suggested that I set goals, put them in writing and display them where I can see them daily.

"Yeah, whatever. I've got goals, I don't need to write them down." That's what I said, and that's what I thought.

How stupid of me!

Written goals work! Once I started writing down my goals and displaying them where I could see them and where my family could see them, I started achieving those goals like clockwork. It's all about making that commitment.

One of the reasons that I am writing this book is to help people like you *not make the mistakes* that I made. Mistakes that seriously delayed my own success. Write down your goals and believe in them. Once you do, you will achieve them. Put them where you have to see them daily, and take the time to review them daily. It will keep you on track and keep you focused on the things that are important.

Your written goals should be specific, not vague. Use actual numbers. If you want a certain amount of net income before the end of this year, write it down. But also write down the strategies that you will employ to achieve that goal.

Here's a technique that really worked for me. I heard actor Jim Carrey tell a similar story on TV. After brainstorming with some like-minded people about goals for the upcoming year, I fixed a number in my head. That was the amount of money I wanted to earn per month. It was quite lofty for me at the time.

I multiplied that number times twelve to come up with the annual income that the number would provide me, and I made out a check, payable to myself, for that amount of money. I signed the check and laminated it to a piece of cardstock. Under the check I detailed exactly what I would have to do in order to achieve my lofty goal. I then hung that piece of laminated cardstock on my computer monitor.

Everybody in the house used the same computer at that time, so they actually had to move my written goal when they wanted to work at the computer. My children were school age at the time, and quite impressionable. I'm sure that my written goal made an indelible impression on their young minds. When they read this book they will recall that piece of laminated cardstock and they will realize, if they haven't already, that the simple technique of a written goal actually worked, since my income is now way beyond the lofty goal I set at that time.

Write yourself a check, laminate it with the action plan you will employ to achieve your goal, and don't be afraid to let others see it. I will do the same. I need a new goal.

Use Every Minute of Every Day for the Most Productive Activity Possible

This is important, and adopting and adhering to this one principle will also put you on the fast track to success.

The average person wastes an incredible amount of time daily. Be productive, have an agenda and follow your agenda. Don't let other people waste your time with non-essential, non-productive nonsense.

Understand what productive is. Work is productive, but working to grow your business is more productive. Most people who own a business go to work every day and work. Work is work, but it's usually not productive. You can hire people to do the work, and you will pay them a lot less than your own time is worth. Your time is best spent finding ways to grow the business and increase your own personal wealth.

Don't waste time! Force yourself to be productive. Being self-employed requires an incredible amount of self-discipline. In the evenings, how much TV do you watch? Stop it! A little TV is fine, it's a good way to

11

unwind, but it can become addictive. There are more important things you can be doing with your time, like reading and working on your business. Even if it's just working on your business mentally.

Is sitting on the porch with your spouse a waste of time? Or playing ball with the kids; is that a waste of time? Absolutely not. Your family is important and you need a good balance of quality family time and work time. Is talking on the phone with your girlfriend for hours at a time a waste of time? Or going to the bar with your buddies? Yes, those things are probably a waste of time if you do them on a regular basis.

Just be conscious of what you are doing at all times. Ask yourself, "Would there be a better way to spend that time?"

A few minutes seem like a really small thing, but if you apply all of these principles on a daily basis you will achieve incredible success. If you spend ten minutes with a pencil and a legal pad brainstorming a new idea for your business and implement that idea the very next day, it could make you an incredible amount of money over the next ten years. Especially if you apply all of the other principles that you will find in this book.

Stop Procrastinating

The world belongs to those who are willing to take immediate action! There is something that you are supposed to be doing. You know what it is. I don't. But it's out there, and you need to get it done. Think about it. Human beings have a knack for creating very complex reasons why they can't do *this* right now. Not until *this is done*.

All of those "reasons" are not reasons. They are excuses. Sometimes it's fear of failure. And even though people won't believe for a minute that fear of failure is the reason for their procrastination, oftentimes it is the very reason they are procrastinating.

Another big roadblock is fear of criticism. As long as people don't know what you are up to, they can't criticize you when it doesn't work. This is a huge problem with a lot of people. Think about it. Think really hard about it. If you secretly fear being criticized by friends, family or peers, you have to get over it.

They criticize you because of their own shortcomings. Because of their own fears, their own failures. You have to learn to trudge ahead and believe in yourself. Let them criticize away . . . in your rearview mirror. If you believe in yourself, and follow the principles in this book and build on those principles, you will succeed and need not fear anything.

Force Yourself to Do the Things You Don't Like to Do

If there is one thing successful people do that other people don't do, it's that they force themselves to do things they'd prefer not to do. What is it that you don't like to do? Make cold calls, offer upsell items to customers, or manage help? Make changes in your business? Implement new ideas and new strategies?

There are at least a few things that you don't like to do. Once you force yourself to do these things, as much as you don't want to do them, you will achieve more success. This idea can be combined with the "stop procrastinating" theory. If you face the fact that you are procrastinating because you don't want to do the things that you should be doing, you can accomplish two of these actions with one effort.

If you tackle each item that you listed on the card, you will eventually see how they all come together to make you incredibly successful in your business.

Have More Entrepreneurial Thoughts

This is important, and it plays a huge part in the title of this book, *Can any Small Business Make You Rich?* The reason that I ask if your small business can make you rich is because any successful small business can provide you with the means and the opportunity to expand your horizons.

In his enlightening book, *The E-myth*, Michael Gerber explains the difference between a typical small business owner and a true entrepreneur. He explains that many people are skilled technicians who are very, very good at what they do, and eventually they start their own businesses doing what it is they are so good at.

Suddenly owning a business isn't as much fun as it was supposed to be, and in many cases it's not nearly as profitable as what they were doing when they were working for someone else. They suddenly find themselves in a world they don't know and don't like.

Most of these people fail to realize that there is a huge difference between being a skilled craftsman and a successful business owner. A business owner must be entrepreneurially-minded and think more along the lines of running the business successfully, and less about doing the "thing" that they do so well.

You must become entrepreneurial. As an entrepreneurial person you will see opportunities that others are completely oblivious to.

Let's say that you run a nice little coffee shop on the corner of 5th and Vine. How many cups of coffee and how many bagels can you sell in a day? How many customers can you serve? What is the highest average transaction amount you can expect in your coffee house?

All of these things have limits. You can only fit so many people in the store at one time by law. You can only serve so many people in an hour no matter how hard you work or how much help you hire. You can only get the average transaction size *this high* no matter what you do.

Your wonderful little coffee shop has its limitations. It can make you only so rich. But a true entrepreneur will get that coffee shop running at full speed without his or her daily efforts, then move on to the next "big idea" on his or her list. While the coffee shop cranks out a steady income, the entrepreneur will be working on income stream number two, or numbers two and three.

If you don't see a steady stream of new business opportunities daily, or other small businesses that you know you could "fix", you are not thinking on an entrepreneurial level. Work on that. Read, read, read. The more you learn about business success and marketing, the more entrepreneurial you will become.

Learn to Time Block

Time blocking is a simple idea which means that you make appointments with yourself. Appointments that cannot be broken, cannot be changed, and cannot be interrupted.

For instance, I have a goal to get this book done by a certain date. I've given myself a deadline and I block out time on my schedule to work on this book. I know at what time of the day I am the most proficient at writing, and I schedule that time to work on this book. I am unavailable to do anything else during the times that I have blocked out to work on this book.

Time blocking is the most powerful means of accomplishing the things that you need to accomplish.

In order to be able to do this effectively, you have to make sure that you build systems into your business. Like McDonald's. Say what you want about McDonald's, but Ray Kroc was a genius at creating and implementing systems. He made running a restaurant so simple that unskilled adults and high school kids can do it with ease, and do it well if they so choose. At McDonald's they have a system for everything they do.

I build systems into my business, which is why my business runs perfectly without my input. I don't take incoming phone calls, I don't take incoming emails, I rarely have to return a phone call, and my assistant responds to 99.5 percent of my emails. My two employees understand what their roles are and they seldom bother me with questions. My customers are trained to know "Mike is unavailable". At first they are puzzled, but they quickly realize that's how it is. Since we still offer incredible value, they happily continue to do business with me.

Most people are under the impression that any business owner should be available at the beck and call of customers, employees and vendors. That's not the way it should work, and you might have to reinvent your business so it does not work that way. Your time as an entrepreneur is far too valuable to spend on meaningless details. But as long as you allow people to have access to you with meaningless questions, it will always be that way. And they will remain dependent on you to help them make even the most meaningless decisions. Train them to be independent thinkers.

Then you can spend your time growing your business and your income.

Understand the 80/20 Rule

There are a lot of variations of the 80/20 rule. Twenty percent of your products account for eighty percent of your sales and so on. But the most important 80/20 rule that you should focus on is this one:

Twenty percent of your customers account for eighty percent of your income.

Think about that. At first you might be inclined to argue with me. Go ahead, it's your business. I'm just pointing out an extremely valuable fact that is true in most small businesses. Even if you cannot attribute eighty percent of your income to twenty percent of your customers, you certainly can discover some important facts about your business if you start looking at your customers as a group, then comparing them to one another.

Ask yourself this question: If there was a state law that allowed me to only have *X* number of customers, and I actually had to drop twenty percent of my customers, how would I choose which ones to drop? I'll bet a few come to mind immediately! But what about the others? How are they different? Are some more valuable than others? Of course they are.

As you do this exercise you should start putting your customers into groups - A, B, C, D, E, – with A being the best customers you have, E being the least valuable, or the highest-maintenance customers you have. All of a sudden it's pretty easy to see which customers you'd drop if you had to.

Now let's focus on the A and B customers. Who are they? Why are they so valuable? How can you find more customers just like them? Where do they live? Is there a hobby or activity that brings them to you? What is their level of income? Do this exercise and plant this seed in your mind. As you get into the marketing section of this book you'll discover how to use this information to attract more customers just like your A and B customers.

How much would your income go up if all of your customers were suddenly just like your A and B customers? It's this kind of critical thinking that separates ultra-successful small business owners from the average small business owner.

Advertise Aggressively!

This is what this book is really about. If you want your small business to bring you riches, then you must enable it to do so. Years ago when I first went into business, I quickly started getting all kinds of referrals from my customers. Before long, 99 percent of all of my work came from referrals. But there was a problem with that. I didn't see the problem at the time, but it was there. This was a service business.

When all of your business comes from referrals, people come to you and tell you exactly how they would like to do business with you. At first I thought this was just fantastic. But as my business evolved, I realized that I didn't want to offer ten different services. I only wanted to offer one service. The one which I could do the most efficiently and turn the jobs over quickly. I knew that I could make a lot more money if I could just concentrate on this one area of my business and say no when people wanted me to do other things.

But how do you tell people that you want to do "this" and not "that"?

23

You create an advertising machine that brings you exactly the kind of customer and the kind of sales you are looking for. They come to you asking for exactly what you want to sell. It's easier than you think.

But you have to get over the fact that advertising costs a lot of money. That's just not true. As you work your way through this book you'll realize that *good advertising* doesn't cost a thing and it can bring you a significant amount of income. Most business owners try to spend as little as possible on advertising, when in fact you should be trying to spend as much as possible on advertising.

If you have a successful advertising campaign that is working well, you should be able to run it on a till forbid basis where it will run continuously on its own until you stop or change it. Always try to find a way to invest more in advertising. If one dollar spent on advertising brings in two, five, ten or twenty dollars in profit, your goal should be to invest as much as possible in advertising. Later in the book I am going to show you how to do that.

Stop the Time Wasters

I already touched on this when I explained the concept of time blocking. Being unavailable when you have time blocked out is a great concept, but allowing people to waste your time at other times chosen by *them* is just plain wrong.

Time is the most valuable asset you have. You've already learned not to waste your time doing things that you can hire someone to do. Now the next step is to make sure as much of your time as possible is available to do the extremely productive things that you should be doing. The things that most small business owners never quite get around to doing.

Once you free up all of this time and start spending a great deal more time on creating super-effective marketing strategies for your business, your business will grow exponentially. That should be your focus, your daily goal.

As you go through your daily routine, start keeping a log of how many times you are interrupted, by whom and why. Before long you will quickly realize who is stealing the most time from you. If it's an employee, they are robbing you twice. When they interrupt you, you not only lose your own valuable time, your train of thought, and probably any momentum that you had going for you, but you also lose the time they are wasting to bother you. If they weren't bothering you, what productive thing could they be doing?

Next you have to ask yourself why they do this. Are you such a control freak that you don't allow them to make decisions on their own? Or in the past have you been exceptionally hard on them when they've made a poor decision?

Years ago as a very young man, I applied for a job with a landscape contractor and on my first day at work this is what he said to me; "Mike, when I am gone I expect you to make decisions. You know a lot about this business, so I am confident that most of the time you will make the right decision. If you make the wrong decision we'll fix it. If I come back to a job site and find all production stopped because you didn't know what to do, I'll fire you. Any questions?" No, I didn't have any questions. He'd made himself perfectly clear!

He also made it perfectly clear that making a wrong decision wasn't such a big deal, and he was confident that any wrong decision I could possibly make could be fixed. What message have you sent to the people who work for you? If you are not giving them room to grow, and demanding that they think for themselves without making it miserable for them when they make a mistake, you are painting yourself into a corner and your business will never be able to grow.

Think about this.

You are the innovator of your business. If you give yourself the freedom to exercise your mind in a peaceful environment, you can innovate and implement on behalf of your business all day long and your business will grow and exceed all of your expectations.

Most small business owners fall into a rut and just start going through the motions of doing their daily "chores". Chores should be left to people who prefer to work by the hour. Your time is better spent brainstorming for new ideas, hidden profit centers in your business and marketing strategies that will bring you a steady stream of new customers.

If you allow others to interrupt you all day long, that will never happen.

Think Bigger!

Read the book, *The Magic of Thinking Big*. It will help you grasp the concept of always thinking bigger. Thinking bigger should be one of your daily goals, because as you go through your days you should always be asking yourself, "Am I thinking as big as possible with this project?" Oftentimes the answer will be no.

Let's say that you are doing a special promotion and you are letting all of your regular customers know, as well as doing some advertising in local media. Can you do more? The answer is yes, you can do more.

Get the media to attend your event and report on it. Make it so interesting and so exciting that they'll want to attend. Make it newsworthy. In the Cleveland area I've had my business featured on TV twice. Once I was in the studio for a daytime show, and the second time they came to my house and did a nice little segment in my backyard. All you have to do is ask!

I once asked a national magazine to *give* me a little space in their magazine, hoping they would respond. Oh boy, did they respond! They ended up paying me six hundred dollars to write an article for the magazine, flew the art director and a professional photographer to my house, gave me four pages inside the magazine, a photo in the table of contents and the entire *front cover of the magazine!*

If you pop into http://TurntheCrankMarketing.com you can download this free report: "The Secret to Tons of Free Publicity for Your Business".

Think bigger.

Deposit into Your Wealth
Account Once a Week

This is huge. If I have one major regret in my business life, it's not implementing this strategy sooner. Why is this such a huge regret for me? Two reasons. One, had I done so, I would have wealth beyond my imagination today. And secondly, even when I was down and out, struggling in business, I still could have squeezed out a weekly deposit into a wealth account.

A wealth account is a separate bank account or an investment account where you put money that can only be used to create wealth for yourself. At the end of each week, before you do anything else, you write yourself a check for your wealth account. You put the money in the account, and the only time you touch it is to move it into something that will give you a greater return on investment.

I won't proclaim to be an investment expert because I am not, and everybody has their own idea about how to best invest their money. The most important thing is that you set some money aside on a weekly basis. The amount that you set aside should be a fixed amount.

Currently I take exactly ten percent of my gross sales at the end of each week and move that amount into my wealth account.

When I first started with my wealth account, one of the things that kept me procrastinating about getting it started was I didn't know what to do with the money, how to invest it. I was interested in the stock market, but didn't fully understand how it worked or how to pick stocks that had the likelihood of appreciating. Then I discovered a simple system for stock picking that seems to be serving me well so far. If you'd like my free report on how I pick really good stocks, just log into http://TurntheCrankMarketing.com to read my free report. It's easy to read and reveals my simple system for stock picking. It's a lot simpler than you think.

If you are like I was, you are not currently depositing into a wealth account because you just can't afford it right now. I am going to tell you a little secret about money. It's like water, it does not have the ability to pile up. You can't shovel it into a pile and expect it to stay there. Money is self-liquidating, especially money that is unaccounted for. Trust me, this is true.

Looking back to my days when I was working really hard in my business just trying to keep my family fed and clothed, I didn't have a lot of extra money. So the thought of setting money aside in a wealth account seemed impossible.

Or was it?

Back when I was in a service business, a typical service call would take me an hour, maybe ninety minutes. The invoice might be $139, with $35 going to parts. That left me a gross profit of $104. Ten percent of the gross would have been $14. Could I have taken that $14 right then and there and put it into a wealth account and still have taken care of my family?

The answer is a resounding yes! But I didn't. Because the block between my ears convinced me that I couldn't afford to invest "right now".

So instead, I just put the money into my checking account where it could "pile up" until I needed it for essential expenses. And of course "pile up" it did not. It simply dissipated.

When I look back at all of the gross income that I failed to take even five or ten percent of and set aside for wealth building, I am not happy with myself. Don't make this mistake. You can afford to take a given percentage each week and put it into your wealth account. At the end of the month you'll never miss it. As a matter of fact, just by doing this wealth-building exercise on a weekly basis you will remind yourself of your other *daily goals*, and that alone will easily more than make up for any money that you deposit into your wealth account.

Years from now you will be quite happy with yourself for adopting the daily disciplines spelled out in this book.

Think Accurately

There are a lot of illusions that surround the world of small business. These illusions are based on thoughts, inaccurate theory, and much propaganda.

Many people in business think, "if I just keep doing what I'm doing, eventually this will pay off big." But how can it pay off big if you haven't intentionally put things in place for it to pay off big?

Other people think that their business is their retirement plan, and when they are ready to kick back and take it easy they'll sell the business and live fat and happy for a very long time. Things change. The market changes. Suddenly you may find yourself surrounded with competition. Or worse yet, whatever it is that you sell is no longer in demand. The new generation could give two hoots about your XYZ Widget.

Your business may quit growing. When a business quits growing, it starts shrinking. I see it all the time. Mainly because the owners of these shrinking businesses did not spend enough time *working on* their business and just "went to work" each day, doing the mundane work of the day.

The time to start making yourself rich is now. That's why I have spelled out the principles of making yourself rich in this book. I've laid out a lot of small and simple business principles. If you strategically employ and apply these principles to your business, you will be able to easily deposit into your wealth account on a weekly basis.

Just one of these principles applied consistently over a period of years can make you a lot of additional money that you would not have earned without the use of the principle. But when you figure out how to apply them all at the same time, and keep them working for you . . . well, let's just say you'll see a big difference in your net profit.

But you have to think accurately and do the right thing with the money as it comes in, and get it into your wealth account where it can start building on its own via passive income.

Accurate thinking means that you have to take each of the principles in this book and find a way to apply them to your business, rather than dismissing them as something that won't work for your business. I am on a mission to prove that these principles can be applied to any business, and I will regularly share case histories of how these principles have been applied to a variety of different businesses. Check out these case histories at http://TurntheCrankMarketing.com. Stop in regularly, your idea machine will be invigorated.

Better yet, tell me how you applied these principles to your business and I'll share your case history with the world.

Join a Mastermind Group

In his incredibly successful book, *Think and Grow Rich*, Napoleon Hill was one of the first to fully explain the incredible power of the "Mastermind Group" as a means of stimulating your creative thinking, and a means of making sure you are thinking accurately.

Having your own business is one of the loneliest feelings in the world. The people who work for you have no idea of the emotional rollercoaster that you are on daily. Friends and family really don't want to hear about you and your issues because they have issues of their own. Not only that, they don't own a business, they don't think like a business owner, and they truly have no idea of what they are talking about when they offer you advice. So when they do give you advice it is probably worthless, or worse yet, dangerous.

You can talk to other business owners, but oftentimes that just turns into a session of whining and complaining about the state of the country and the economy.

A mastermind group is different. The sole purpose of a mastermind group is for like-minded people to gather, brainstorm new ideas for each other, share marketing principles, share and transfer knowledge, and genuinely try to help one another reach higher levels of success in business.

A mastermind group is where you can have other business-savvy people look at your ads and sales letters, and offer suggestions and critique. The outcome of every mastermind meeting is always incredibly powerful for those who participate.

One of my primary goals in writing this book is to establish mastermind groups all over the United States and Canada where small business owners can discuss, strategize, and help each other implement "Turn the Crank Marketing" principles that are "vending machine predictable".

I can't even begin to tell you how much value I personally have received by participating in mastermind groups. A single sentence uttered in a mastermind setting could easily be worth $50,000 to you or me, if we are paying attention. I'm serious. I can think of at least two specific instances where somebody else, who might have been somewhat familiar with what I do, uttered a single sentence that made me look at my business differently and change just a few small things, and in doing so increased my net profit by $50,000 or more over time.

The value you receive from a mastermind setting is priceless.

This strategy will make more sense to you as you get further into this book. But for right now, I encourage you to go to http://TurntheCrankMarketing.com and see if you can locate a mastermind group in your area and get involved immediately.

Tap Every Knowledge Base You Can

I achieved my expertise as a marketer via a very indirect path. I was like a lot of other small business owners, struggling to make my way in the business world. Right after starting my first full-time business, I came upon some very difficult economic times and I went through some ugly financial difficulties. But they say that every cloud has a silver lining, and mine sure did.

During that era of my life I accidentally discovered a super-successful means of promoting my business. A way that actually brought me exactly the kind of customers that I wanted to serve. However, I had no idea how or why this new advertising mechanism that I was using worked. The only thing that I knew for sure was that it worked incredibly well, but I was afraid to change any part of it because I didn't know which part made it work.

So eventually I decided to see if I could figure out why this thing was working, and off to the public library I went to find a book on advertising.

That trip to the library changed my life forever, just as I hope reading this book will do for you. I became an advertising, marketing, small business, success junkie, reading every book I could, listening to audio recordings constantly, watching videos, subscribing to every newsletter I could get my hands on.

I am going to attempt to list the authors that I've studied, but I know dozens will escape me. I've been on this quest for twenty-two years. So here's a partial list of the people who have influenced my success, in no particular order . . .

John Caples, Victor Schwab, Jack Canfield, Mark Victor Hanson, Robert Collier, Napoleon Hill, Claude Hopkins, Ben Suarez, Melvin Powers, Russ Von Hoelscher, Richard Benson, E. Joseph Cossman, Joe Sugarman, Jerry Buchanan, Harold Moe, Joe Karbo, Gary Halbert, Dan Kennedy, Jeff Paul, Robert Ringer, Ted Nicholas, Dr. Norman Vincent Peale, Rita Davenport, Tom Hopkins, John Reese, Yanik Silver, Leo Quinn, John David Bradshaw, Ken Silver, Gordon Alexander, Michael Gerber, Joe Polish, Bill Meyers, Dr. Jeffery Lant, John Carlton, Michael LeBoeuf, Steven K. Scott, Roy Hollister Williams, William Carruthers, Brad Antin, Alan Antin, Nicholas Bade, Frank Bettger, Jeff Gardner, T.J. Rohleder, Don Bice, Cynthia Kersey, David Deutsch, Steve Chandler, Sam Beckford, Michael Levine, Stan Golomb, Seth Godin, Jay Abraham, Robert Allen, David Oglivy and Roger Griffith.

Start building your own list of success-minded people to study.

Getting Your Mind Around the Small Business Vending Machine Strategy

This is the essence of "Turn the Crank Marketing".

Just for a moment, consider this scenario:

You have a vending machine in the lobby area of your business. This vending machine does not dispense cans of soda, candy bars or peanut butter crackers. Instead, the machine dispenses little plastic eggs, each containing a *twenty dollar bill!*

You drop in a one dollar bill, turn the crank, and out drops a little plastic egg containing a twenty dollar bill.

What would you do?

You'd do the same thing that I or any other normal person would do. You'd visit the vending machine as often as you could. More than likely you would just keep going back all day long until the machine was out of little plastic eggs and twenty dollar bills.

As crazy as this sounds, the strategy that you are about to discover is almost that simple. My area of expertise is in creating marketing systems for small businesses that bring in new business almost as predictably as the scenario I just described to you.

Of course, as they say, there is no such thing as a free lunch. So I am not going to make outlandish, ridiculous claims that are too good to be true. Instead I am going to share with you techniques and strategies that you can apply to your business that will make your marketing "vending machine predictable".

The strategies that I teach work. I've used them over and over and over since 1983. I've been studying small business marketing for over twenty-three years and it pains me to see small business owners spending their hard-earned money on marketing that either isn't working at all, or just barely turning out enough business to recover the cost of the marketing.

I've talked to countless business owners who've told me, "I've tried that kind of advertising and it just doesn't work for my kind of business." Of course they believe that to be true, but in reality that statement is completely untrue. I'm about to prove to you why it's untrue, and what changes to make so your marketing is "vending machine predictable".

"Vending machine predictable" means that you can invest a given amount of money in marketing your business and know with a reasonable degree of certainty that you are going to get a predictable return on investment.

Slide a dollar into your marketing machine and pull out twenty dollars. Slide two dollars into your marketing machine and pull out forty dollars. Of course there are a lot of variables involved in different businesses, so I cannot guarantee you a given amount of return on investment.

But I promise that if you employ the strategies that you are about to discover, you will see a marked difference in how predictable your marketing will become.

Read this manual carefully.

It could change your business and your life forever.

When I first started in business years ago, I thought I knew how to market my business and I thought I was good at it.

Those were foolish thoughts.

It would be years later before I would accidentally discover that I could actually control when and how I would get new customers, and I could actually control *what kind of customers* I would get.

Consider that for a moment. You can actually control who calls or comes into your business. When your business starts to slow down a little, you turn the crank and kick in your marketing machine.

Yes, I first made the discovery of "effective marketing" by accident. That was 1983. I didn't solve the puzzle by any means. I just realized that marketing done correctly can and will bring very predictable results.

It was that accidental discovery that sent me on a twenty-three-year mission of the study of effective marketing. I learned a lot about marketing, and applied what I learned to what I was doing and my results just got better and better.

But I'm almost embarrassed to admit that it would be years later before I actually figured out what it was about that accidental discovery which made that one little advertisement incredibly effective.

You won't have to wait years to figure it out.

I am going to explain it to you here, and explain how important this one little strategy is to establishing super-effective marketing for your business. If you only apply one strategy of the many that you are about to discover in this manual, the one strategy that eluded me for so long will make your marketing "vending machine predictable".

Okay, let's get started.

The Lifetime Value of a Customer

This is one of the most important things for you to understand in order for you to effectively evaluate any marketing strategy that you employ.

How much is a new customer worth to your business?

Really. In dollars and cents, what is the exact amount of money that each new customer represents to your business? That's a number you should know. A number that is foremost in your mind every single day while you work to run your business.

I know exactly what you are thinking; "That's impossible. You can't put a value on a customer, all customers are different."

That may be true, all customers are different. But you really need to study your business and figure out how much money your average customer spends with you in a year. That's a pretty easy number to put together. Spend some time on it, set up a system of tracking it so you can not only establish this number, but so you can adjust the number constantly as your business evolves.

The next thing you need to do is determine how long a customer does business with you before going away. Is it one year, two years, five years? How long does *the average person* do business with you once they start giving you money?

For instance, Dan is my auto mechanic. I started doing business with Dan about two years ago. On average I have been spending about $2,500 per year with Dan since I started doing business with him. Since I have been quite pleased with him for over two years now, I think it would be very realistic to say that I will continue doing business with Dan for at least another three years.

So I spend $2,500 per year with Dan and will likely do business with Dan for five years. As an example, let's assume that I am average for a "Dan customer". That means that the lifetime value of a customer for Dan is $10,000.

I like Dan so much that I told my sister-in-law about Dan, and since they also have three vehicles to maintain, I'm sure that they too will spend about the same amount with him that I do. So the average is actually a reasonable number to use.

So we've determined that Dan's average customer has a lifetime value of $10,000. That's a lot of money! For just a minute let's assume that we are wrong, and maybe that number is only fifty percent of what I think it is. That's $5,000. That's still a lot of money.

Based on these figures of either $10,000 or $5,000, how much do you think that Dan can afford to spend to attract a new customer? Let's use the lower number and assume that on each job, Dan has a net profit of fifty percent of the invoice price. That means that each new customer that Dan gets is worth $2,500 in net profit.

So even if Dan spent as much as $1,000 to attract a new customer to his business, he'd still be $1,500 to the good in the long run. But Dan doesn't have to spend anywhere near $1,000 to attract a new customer. He can probably attract a new customer for as little as $50 in actual marketing costs.

Let's assume that Dan can create a marketing strategy that brings in new customers on a steady basis, and at the end of each week he counts to see how many new customers his marketing system brought in. He then divides that number into the actual cost of the marketing for the week.

In other words, let's say that he spends $500 on either a newspaper ad or a postcard that is designed to get people to visit his repair shop for the first time. At the end of the week he has ten new customers for the week. That's a cost of $50 per customer, and each customer represents a potential net profit of $2,500.

What should Dan do? He should keep using that marketing tool on a forever basis! It's bringing him a steady flow of high-value customers.

Now at the end of the month when Dan gets his $2,000 advertising bill (four weeks times $500) he no longer has to get all nervous about writing that big check, thinking the money is wasted, because he knows that for $2,000 he just bought *forty new customers*, each one worth $2,500.

That is what I call making your marketing "vending machine predictable".

You can make any business or practice – yes, I said 'any business *or practice*' – "vending machine predictable". If you use this manual, you will make your business or practice "vending machine predictable".

When you actually know the lifetime value of a customer or a client and you couple that knowledge with the marketing savvy you will discover in this manual, your business or practice can skyrocket.

I don't care if you are a doctor, a dentist, a chiropractor or a pig farmer, this manual will make your business or practice "vending machine predictable" if you use it.

If you use it . . .

You have to adapt to what you are about to learn to your particular business, but it can and will work.

If you don't use it, shame on you!

Read this manual over and over. You'll discover something new each time you read it.

The Unique Selling Proposition

Every business or practice should have a Unique Selling Proposition?

"A what?"

A Unique Selling Proposition is a marketing strategy that completely sets you apart from your competition and gives potential customers a powerful reason to do business with you for the very first time.

I know you are going to fight me on this for a number of reasons. One, you are far too professional to use a stupid gimmick to attract customers. But the real reason that you are going to fight me on this is because it is going to take really deep thought and action. Oh yeah, and it also takes "cajones" to implement a powerful Unique Selling Proposition.

Cajones? Yeah, you know, broad shoulders and a strong backbone to stand behind what you believe in. Too many business people want to be namby-pamby trying to please everybody, then complain to anybody who will listen about how terrible business is.

Business is what you make it!

Make yours incredibly successful with a powerful Unique Selling Proposition.

Your business needs a powerful Unique Selling Proposition, one that is so powerful that potential customers will do what they normally would not do to do business with you.

For instance, all tax accountants pretty much offer the same service. They file this form, that form, do this, do that, blah blah blah. In other words, they all look the same, so just pick one.

You have to make sure your business doesn't look and sound the same. Stand out in the crowd! No matter how boring you think your business is, you can make it exciting with a powerful Unique Selling Proposition. Don't be plain vanilla in a world full of plain vanilla. *Be Outrageous Raspberry!*

Let's look at some examples:

Just a few days ago I looked into buying a small business that has been in this town for as long as I can remember, and I've been here for fifty years. At one time this was a very viable, profitable little ice cream store. But over the years it has been sold a number of times, and even though one owner did make some positive improvements, he did not follow through with good business practices.

In short, this business is once again for sale, but it no longer has a record of being a profitable business. Nonetheless, I know the place has enormous potential. I'm really not that excited about running the business, but I know I could turn it around and make it a very profitable little enterprise.

I've been thinking about this place for a long time, and chances are I won't buy it simply because I am too busy with my other ventures. But mentally I have completely reinvented this plain-vanilla ice cream store into a fun-filled destination that will pull customers in from at least 25 miles away.

It has never before attracted customers from more than a few miles. How could it? You can find a "regular" ice cream store every few miles. Why travel to one?

Think about that; taking your business from a marketing radius of 2.5 miles to 25 miles. Do you realize how many more prospective customers that would be?

That's a bold statement, I know, but of the many things that I would do to turn this business around, I would give it a Unique Selling Proposition!

More about that in a minute, but first let's start with the basics. The first thing that I would do would be to change the name from the plain-vanilla ice cream store name that it's had for years. The new name would be Pinky's Burger Joint.

Has an interesting ring to it, doesn't it? Not a restaurant, not a hamburger stand, but a "burger joint". And not just any burger joint, but . . .
Pinky's Burger Joint.

Calling the place a joint instead of a restaurant makes it interesting, bold, and curious.

So who is Pinky, you might ask? Pinky is just a fictional character that I've dreamed up to add more curiosity to the experience of eating at Pinky's. Did you notice that I described a visit to Pinky's as an experience?

A visit to your business should also be an experience. It should be memorable to the point that people talk about it at work the next day.

More than likely, I would have an artist create a character of this Pinky person. In my mind, Pinky is a big brute, somewhat unshaven and in a cook's uniform, but known the world over for his incredible burgers.

Done correctly, people would feel a very personal connection to this invented fictional character. Most people would actually think this is a real person, even though no effort would be made to make them think that.

Betty Crocker is not a real person and look at the impact she has made on the world.

The next thing that I would do is to paint all of the picnic tables at Pinky's with high gloss paint, hot pink in color. I would also paint the outside of the restaurant high-gloss white trimmed with a lot of high-gloss hot pink.

I'd then hire a neon-sign company to come in and completely trim out the restaurant with hot pink, and maybe purple, neon lighting. This little ice cream store is in a rural area on a very busy highway. For the most part the area is pretty dark at night, and no other businesses are in the immediate area.

Pinky's all trimmed out in neon would be like a beacon in the night!

Behind this little ice cream store there is a little miniature golf course. Not much to look at, but it's there. I'd change that with lots of interesting and neatly maintained landscaping, and more pink and purple neon.

I'd trim out the gardens around the golf course with many interesting and expensive plants with descriptive signs telling what the plants are, and where the original specimen of each plant was discovered or developed. Things like the Lavender Twist Weeping Redbud tree that was found growing wild in a flowerbed in upstate New York, and many different kinds of Japanese Maples.

Why?

Why would I go to all of that trouble to enhance a miniature golf course at an ice cream store? Just to give people one more reason to stay longer, buy more, talk about Pinky's the next day at work and to come back often to visit the gardens.

The next improvement would be a good sound system with plenty of 50s and 60s rock 'n' roll playing all day and evening all around the restaurant, as well as in the miniature golf area.

Are you beginning to get a visual of Pinky's Burger Joint?

The menu?

A handful of tasty burger options. Hot dogs, foot-long hot dogs and Coney dogs, killer coleslaw, and the standard ice cream treats.

Keep it simple and do it well.

The atmosphere? Happy times with happy employees who are hired as much for their dancing skills as their customer service skills. The employees would be encouraged and expected to break into dance at any opportunity, briefly dancing with willing customers as they make their way around the grounds of the restaurant.

Getting a hamburger becomes a memorable experience at Pinky's. People talk about "experiences" at work with the neighbors over the fence, with friends and family via email. Pinky's would become nationally known in a relatively short period of time.

People may not come from around the country to eat at Pinky's, but they would know about Pinky's. Pretty soon the community begins to take ownership of Pinky's. The place is famous, and it's in "our" backyard.

I'd have to say that at least six or seven generations have been to this ice cream store over the years, so when you take a place like this that was once thriving and breathe new and fresh life into it, people will tell their friends, family and siblings, recall the "good ol' days" and tell them how much fun it is now. This kind of viral marketing is priceless.

Viral marketing is a relatively new term that is normally associated with the internet, but it can work for brick and mortar businesses as well. Viral marketing spreads like a virus, whether you want it to or not.

With these changes, in a matter of months the once unknown plain-vanilla ice cream store has become a destination and an experience.

Pay attention here, I'm going to give you a priceless piece of information that, if you use it to your advantage, you can launch your business to the next level.

Henry David Thoreau said, "Most men live quiet lives of desperation." Of course his quote is dated, but still true. The truth is *most people* live quiet lives of desperation.

When you can create an experience for them as I have done here with Pinky's, at least conceptually, they will love you forever and not even know why.

Make your business a destination people will talk about! Get creative, it can be done.

And guess what?

We haven't even gotten to the Unique Selling Proposition (USP) that I've come up with for Pinky's. See my newspaper advertisement on the next page:

Ice Cream Cones only 15¢

Yes, we actually sell ice cream cones for 15¢! No gimmicks, no gags. Real cold and creamy ice cream cones only 15¢ each! Choose from chocolate, vanilla, or the flavor of the week. The flavor of the week is a secret, you have to come out and see what the flavor of the week is. Okay, so these 15¢ ice cream cones are not great big pack-the-fat-on-your-hips ice cream cones, but for 15¢ you'll be impressed. If you feel cheated, just ask for your money back. There! How's that? A Money Back Guarantee on a 15¢ ice cream cone. You can't beat that with a stick!

Okay, so that's the deal. 15¢ ice cream cones. Now grab Mama, get in the car and come out and get yourself one of our 15¢ ice cream cones. Come on, you ain't doin' nothin' anyway. Now get in the dag blamed car!

Oh yeah, we also got a miniature golf course here at **Pinky's**. We'll let ya play a round of golf for a nickel. That's right, a round of minature golf for 5¢! Bring a quarter and we'll give you an ice cream cone, a round of golf, and a nickel back. Now grab Mama and get in the dag blamed car! We're on Route 20 in Madison. If you're comin' from the west we're on the right, if you're comin' from the east were on the left, and if you're comin' from the north we're straight ahead. Why in the &^$# you'd be comin' from the north I don't know, but if you are, we're straight ahead. **Pinky's Burger Joint, 1234 North Ridge Road, Madison, Ohio.** (Cut this ad out right now 'cause you'll forget who we are and where we are, and you're gonna have a hankerin for one of our 15¢ ice cream cones.) -- Love, Pinky

I know what you're thinking. What kind of an idiot would sell ice cream cones for fifteen cents when everybody else is charging one dollar or more? First of all, it doesn't cost much to make an ice cream cone, so at fifteen cents I might be able to break even. But even if I lost a few pennies on every cone I sold, it would still be a great idea.

First, let's consider how an offer like this actually allows me to leverage my advertising dollars. I have a new business, so I have to advertise to let people know we're here and why they should care. Let's say that each time I run the ad I've created, the newspaper charges me $300. My goal is to get people to come and "experience" Pinky's. So the only thing I need the ad to do is get people to show up.

I could run a namby-pamby ad telling people about Pinky's, but without giving them a powerful reason to come out, we're only going to get X number of people to show up. Or we can run the ad I've created and make the fifteen-cent ice cream cone offer, and we can easily get five times, ten times, or twenty times X number of people to show up.

Now consider the return on investment from my newspaper ad. The reason that I'm running the ad is to get people to show up and "experience" Pinky's. At this point I'm not even concerned with how much they'll spend, but I'm sure they'll spend more than enough. But for right now all I want is a head count. X number of people. Therefore the return on investment from my advertising will be calculated by dividing the number of people who show up into the cost of the advertisement.

A $300 advertisement divided by 25 people showing up means that it cost $12 for each new customer the ad brings in. But if the fifteen-cent ice cream cone ad brings in 250 people, the cost of a new customer goes down to $1.20 each.

Now remember, Pinky's is unique, it's interesting and it's fun. People are going to tell their friends, family and co-workers about Pinky's. So which is better? Twenty-five people talking about Pinky's, or 250 people talking about Pinky's.

The concept of Pinky's Hamburger Joint is built around word of mouth advertising and the Rule of 250, which says that every person knows and has contact with 250 other people. But you have to set this word of mouth advertising into motion. So if you can create an advertisement and an offer that will put 250 people into motion telling others about you, as opposed to just 25 people, you are actually able to leverage your advertising dollars by the factor of ten, and those numbers will grow exponentially.

Each and every time you run that advertisement and bring in new faces, the numbers will grow exponentially. It's an amazing concept!

What you just read is a Unique Selling Proposition that brings people in, makes them leave happy, and forces them to tell others about your business.

That's your new goal. To create an offer and a Unique Selling Proposition that will do that for your business.

I can hear you now. "Yeah Mike, that's real nice. But I don't sell ice cream cones and hamburgers. I sell hydraulic valves." Be patient, we'll get to those of you in non-retail businesses.

Okay, now let's get back to Pinky's and how you go from selling fifteen-cent ice cream cones to actually making money.

First, let's consider an important fact about human nature. Many people feel guilty about going out to get an ice cream cone. As sad as it is, it's true. To many people, ice cream is a bad thing that only weak-minded souls indulge in. But oftentimes only one person in a relationship actually thinks that way.

So from that point of view, how much damage can a fifteen-cent ice cream cone do? This fifteen-cent ice cream cone advertisement will pull in people who normally would not be pulled in by the typical banana-split-dripping-with-sauces ad. So by using this concept we have broadened our potential customer base.

Next: People are people are people are people.

They come to Pinky's because we promised them a fifteen-cent ice cream cone, but once they are on the lot many of them will opt to spend more. Some will decide to get a burger and fries and have the ice cream cone for dessert. Others will order milkshakes, sundaes and other treats. Some will only buy the fifteen-cent ice cream cone, but they are likely to come back again, and they are likely to tell others about Pinky's and the fifteen-cent ice cream cones.

Then there's the law of reciprocity that says when you give somebody something, they feel compelled to do something kind for you in return. If you give them a great deal on a fifteen-cent ice cream cone, many will feel compelled to buy something else just so they don't feel they are taking advantage.

People really do think that way. Actually, most people feel that way. They really don't know that's how they respond, but marketing test after marketing test has proven it to be true.

So to recap the Unique Selling Proposition and marketing strategy of Pinky's Hamburger Joint, here it is in a nutshell:

1. Unique, colorful, friendly and pleasant buying experience at Pinky's.
2. Powerful advertisement with an attention-grabbing headline.
3. Extremely strong offer that's really hard to ignore. Fifteen-cent ice cream cones!
4. Strong call to action in the advertisement. "Now grab Mama and get in the dag blamed car!"
5. Powerful use of the Rule of 250. Everybody knows 250 people. Give them a reason to tell those 250 people about Pinky's.
6. A marketing plan that is "vending machine predictable". Run the advertisement, new people show up, those new people tell the 250 people they know, next week more new people show up, those new people tell the 250 people they know.

More About Unique Selling Propositions

The very first, yet extremely powerful Unique Selling Proposition that I ever used I discovered by accident. At the time I didn't even know what a Unique Selling Proposition was and it would be years later before I would grasp the concept to the point that I understood it.

As you are reading this now, you have a huge advantage in discovering the concept of a Unique Selling Proposition, and if you really work at it you can create a powerful USP for your business.

So how powerful is this USP concept?

This is the very first USP that I accidentally developed:

"Your House Re-Landscaped only $495"

Looks kind of simple, doesn't it? Actually it looks kind of dumb. Not if you know what it accomplished. But here's the most important thing that it did right out of the gate.

The very first advertisement I ran using this headline pulled in new business at a rate of *33.3 times ad cost!*

Think about that. The advertisement cost me $150 and I sold $5,000 worth of new business!

I couldn't believe it! Never had I run an advertisement that even came close to that. The first time I ran the ad, it ran in a coupon-type book that went to 20,000 homes. Unfortunately the guy doing the coupon book went out of business after the first issue. But I was onto something, and over the years I tweaked the ad and ran it over and over for *fifteen years* in the local newspaper. The return on investment remained at a steady twenty times ad cost each time the ad ran.

Think about what twenty times ad cost really means. It means that I invested $200 in a newspaper ad, and as a direct result of that investment did $4,000 worth of new business with people whom I had never met before.

But actually this USP did a lot more for me than just getting a high rate of return of ad cost. At the time my landscaping business was a part-time venture and I only wanted to do business with a certain kind of customer. I wanted absolutely nothing to do with landscaping new homes.

I had been in that market and it was so fiercely competitive that I was always bidding against nine or ten competitors. Guess who was in control? The prospective customer, that's who! They were smart; they'd work one bidder against another trying to get the most bang for their buck. Good for them, bad for those trying to earn a living by landscaping new homes.

Out of pure desperation, I accidentally discovered the USP that would forever change the way I would do business. Since the headline and all of the body copy in my advertisement talked about "re-landscaping" homes, new home owners did not call. That was perfectly fine with me. I'd had enough of that market!

Not only did the accidental discovery of my very own Unique Selling Proposition completely reinvent my business and the way I did business, it sent me on a more than twenty-year quest to always find the next level for myself personally and professionally. Had I not accidentally made that discovery back in 1983, my life would be very different today and I don't think I'd be very happy with it.

Make it your personal goal to exploit every opportunity in your business and your life, starting today. Apply the principles that you are discovering in this book.

Who Do You Want to Do Business With?

Don't tell me "everybody"!!!

You cannot effectively market to everybody. You have to define your ideal customer and picture them in your mind. More about that later, but pay attention to why that is so important and how it helped me.

My very successful landscaping advertisement actually quoted a price, something that no one else in the business had ever done, nor has anyone done so since I quit running my ads. People with big, expensive homes did not call. I didn't want to do business with them. I only wanted to work for a very specific type of customer; working class people with moderately priced homes.

This is important, pay attention here.

I only wanted to work for working class people with moderately priced homes.

Through prior experience I knew the "who" I wanted to work for, and with that in mind, I "accidentally" crafted an advertisement that would bring them to me on a steady basis, making it "vending machine predictable".

Keep that in mind. I first established "who" I wanted to do business with.

Of course, at the time I had no idea how sophisticated my strategy was. I was just stumbling along trying desperately to make a living. But I had made a discovery, it worked, and it worked really, really well.

Yes, I was kind of fussy about "who" I wanted to work for. But there are only so many hours in a day, and for my business that particular market was where I could maximize my profits. The jobs were quick and easy to do, the people were very easy and pleasant to work for, and they *always* paid Johnny-on-the-spot as soon as the job was done. That's what I wanted.

By crafting my advertisement as I did, with the powerful Unique Selling Proposition that I was using, the exact type of customer I wanted to work for were the people who responded to my ads. My advertisement did such a great job of pre-qualifying and pre-selling my prospects, that by the time I got to their homes all I had to do was convince them that I really could deliver on what I advertised.

I sold at least three out of every five homeowners who I spoke with, probably closer to four out of every five.

Think about that. I went from bidding against eight or nine competitors for every job and sacrificing a great deal of profit just to get the jobs, to selling sixty to eighty percent of the people I talked to. And the actual sales process was ten times simpler than what I had to go through with new homes.

It was like shooting fish in a barrel!

Here's the ad that started it all . . .

Landscape Renovation
Only $495.00
With Coupon
Reg. Price
$700.00 to $800.00
No Gimmicks - Check Ref.

Hi Folks, I'm Duston,
Me and my Dad want to tear out those old unsightly shrubs around your house and re-landscape with some real pretty ones. Dad says he can do the entire job for only $495.00 if you use this coupon. Give Dad a call and he'll give you a no obligation, formal proposal and breakdown of exactly what you will get for $495.00.

McGroarty Landscape & Concrete
Perry, Ohio   Phone: ▓▓▓▓▓▓▓▓▓▓

Dear Reader, this "dumb" advertisement changed my life forever, just as this book can yours if you take action and apply what you are learning here.

The price in the above ad was way too low, but at the time the nursery-stock market was soft and I could buy plants for almost pennies on the dollar. Over the years as I learned more about how to create a powerful advertisement, I changed the ad and raised the price to almost triple the price shown here. I made tens of thousands of dollars running these ads.

But the most important lesson I learned from running this ad out of sheer desperation, was that small ads can be extremely profitable. I eventually learned that you have to make an irresistible offer in your ads, and that you have to have a Unique Selling Proposition. It cost me $150 to run this ad and it returned $5,000 worth of new business.

That works out to a return on investment of 33.3 times ad cost. That is the art of leveraging your advertising dollars. More about that in a minute.

Think about this!

You really can choose who you want to do business with, and do so on your terms, not theirs.

Don't confuse a USP with a lame slogan like "We're the best cleaner in town." That's not a USP. It's an empty promise of pretty much nothing.

For those of you in the business-to-business or industrial markets, come up with something that really and truly means something to your prospective customers:

Guaranteed widgets in stock when you call, or we'll buy you and your guest a steak dinner at the best restaurant in town.

Or . . .

Never get caught in the voice-mail trap when you call. We guarantee you'll talk with a live sales rep on your first call and every call.

What is it about your industry that is currently driving prospective customers crazy? Fix it and turn it into your USP. Don't know? Conduct a survey and find out!

Leverage Your Advertising Dollars!

It's really important that you grasp this concept of leveraging your advertising dollars. Let's say that you run a newspaper advertisement at a cost of $200 and it brings in $600 worth of new business. Not bad, right? That's three times ad cost. But what if you changed the offer, changed the headline, used a few different words in the ad and suddenly got a very different result?

Instead of your $200 advertisement bringing in $600, suddenly it brings in $4,000. The ad is exactly the same size as it was before, it's placed in the same media, the same circulation, the same cost. The only thing that is different is what the ad says, and how it says it.

Imagine that. A $200 advertisement that usually brings in $600 suddenly brings in $4,000. How often would you run the new version of your advertisement? I hope you answer, "As often as they let me!"

That's what I mean when I say "create a marketing strategy that is vending machine predictable and run it on autopilot". Just let it run nonstop, bringing in a steady flow of new business from people you've never seen before, and people who never even knew you existed until now.

If you are doing all of the other things in your business that you should be doing which turn customers into raving fans, your business will grow exponentially. Once you create a marketing plan for your business that is "vending machine predictable", you will be on your way to incredible success.

A powerful Unique Selling Proposition can help you leverage your advertising dollars and create a marketing strategy that is "vending machine predictable".

Now, I want you to consider this scenario, and this does apply to your business if you really pay attention here.

The lesson is powerful, and a true story.

A guy who likes to grow small plants in his backyard wants to start selling his plants from home. His cost to grow a small plant is only 25 cents and that includes the plastic container and the potting soil. So even if he only charges $4 each for his plants, his margin of profit is still very high.

But . . . the price is still only $4 and advertising space in the newspaper is quite expensive.

To make this situation even more challenging, this man lives in a town that actually has more than one hundred wholesale nurseries growing and selling millions and millions of dollars worth of nursery stock each year. Just a mile away on the main road into town there are five full-service garden centers, all selling plants, all competing for the same business.

Just a short distance away there is a Walmart store, a Kmart, a Lowes and a Home Depot, plus several other retail garden centers, all selling plants, all competing for the same business. All of these retail businesses are spending thousands and thousands of dollars on advertising space in the local newspapers, not to mention television and radio advertising.

How in the world can a guy selling a few plants from home possibly compete in this business arena?

The answer is simple. He created a powerful offer, and a Unique Selling Proposition and . . .

An advertisement that worked so well he got *twenty times return on ad cost!* That's $20 for each dollar invested in advertising.

Think about that. A guy selling a few plants from home, competing in what most would consider a vicious market, runs not one, but several ads and gets a return on investment in advertising dollars of twenty to one.

Think about that twenty to one in real money. An ad that costs $200 brings in $4,000 worth of new business!

And get this! On a product that sold for only four dollars! That's it, just four dollars.

Most people wouldn't dare run a newspaper advertisement for a four-dollar product, being too afraid of completely losing their shirt. Here's the ad:

$4.00 Plant Sale!

We are over stocked, 1,124 plants must be sold. **Every plant is priced at just $4.00 and must be sold this weekend!** Choose from Fragrant Snowball Viburnum, Blue Boy/Girl Holly, Burning Bush, Pink Flowering Weigela, Red Flowering Weigela, Boxwood, Annabelle Hydrangea, Gold Flame Spirea, Cranberry Cotoneaster, Coral Beauty Cotoneaster, Variegated Hosta, Stella D'Oro Daylilly, Japanese Holly, Gold Drop Potentilla, Red Twig Dogwood, Emerald Green Arborvitae, Golden Globe Arborvitae, Blue Rug Juniper, Blue Chip Juniper, Blue Star Juniper, Forsythia, Ornamental Grasses, Variegated Euonymus and more. **McGroarty's Backyard Nursery**ﯹﯹﯹﯹﯹﯹﯹﯹﯹﯹ Ridge Rd., Perry, Ohio 9:00 a.m. to 4:00 p.m. Thursday, Friday, Saturday, and Sunday.

Yeah, this was also my advertisement. This ad worked so well that each spring we completely sold out of plants and had to close our sales even before the spring buying rush was over.

74

But here's the lesson in all of this. As business owners, you and I have a simple, but often difficult job to do. We need to make new friends, bring new faces into our businesses on a daily basis so they can "experience" doing business with us. You have to find a mechanism that will bring new people into your business on a steady basis. A mechanism that is "vending machine predictable".

These little ads did that for us. Each year our business grew and grew because we made more new friends, and the friends we had made over the previous years came back and bought from us over and over. These little ads were "vending machine predictable".

So much so that I now teach this same concept to other small growers around the United States, Canada, England, Ireland, Australia and who knows where else. They too get predictable results with impressive return-on-ad-cost figures.

Your job is to now look at your business differently, and find out what it is about your business that you can use to create a marketing strategy that will be "vending machine predictable". It's there, you just have to look for it. It may take some brainstorming, but it's worth it.

There isn't a business on the planet that cannot use the many strategies that you are discovering in this course. You need to establish a Unique Selling Proposition that truly is so unique and powerful that it means something to your prospective customers.

Okay, now before we move on I might as well show you the ad that ended it all:

Nothing lasts forever, and after selling thousands and thousands of small plants each spring, we decided we'd had enough and had to devote more time to other business interests. By then we had raised the price to $4.97. I created this ad for our final sale and ran it for a period of four weeks with some minor changes each week. In four weeks this ad sold $26,000 worth of $4.97 plants, which gave the ad a return on investment of 28 times ad cost . To this day I am still impressed!

My friend, this is important for you to understand about a strategy like this. Over the years I had sold all kinds of nursery stock; big trees, small trees, flowers, you name it. But for the last few years that we were growing, we opted to only sell $4.97 plants simply because I was tired of lifting and carrying larger plants.

Once again, I had decided who I wanted to do business with and designed my business and my marketing around that customer.

But . . . these little ads can be so much more powerful if you think it through, and I teach this strategy to my plant-growing customers. If you look closely at the ad you'll see that I'm advertising Japanese Red Maples for $4.97. Japanese Red Maples are one of the most popular plants in the plant kingdom and they often sell for as much as $500 each. It's not unusual to find them in the garden centers for $300 to $500, and it's really rare to find them priced below $100. But I was selling them for $4.97, and as I write this I've got growers around the country selling them for $4.97.

Of course they are small, and they are not the most expensive variety on the market, but they are still Japanese Red Maples for only $4.97 and people jump at the chance to buy them for that price. But I also learned that if you set a $150 Laceleaf Weeping Japanese Red Maple right next to your $4.97 Japanese Red Maples, some customers will buy two small ones and one $150 tree and be happy to have had the chance to do so.

And this is where garden centers around the country lack the *cajones* to use this powerful strategy. Instead they just keep doing what they've always done, but for some reason it doesn't work as well as it used to.

The reason that it doesn't work as well as it used to is because along came all of the big box stores, and lots and lots of people buy plants from them. People really don't want to buy plants at the big box stores because they really like going to independently-owned garden centers, but the garden centers refuse to use the necessary appeal to get them on the lot.

Instead, what the garden center industry did as a whole was to quit selling low-priced plants because that was a cheesy market that belonged to the big box stores. At least that's what they seem to think.

Hello?

Independently-owned garden centers are going out of business like crazy. I wonder why?

Folks, you have to adapt to the changing market or get left in the dust. Big box stores are very easy to compete with. They do a lot of things wrong and they can't help it. They are just too big to control everything.

Find out what it is they are really messing up and exploit that particular area in your own business. Your customers will love you for it.

I recently did an advertisement critique for a customer. I want to share with you the changes that I suggested so you can apply some of the same principles to your own advertising.

When designing an advertisement, you really have to think about the prospect and try to enter the conversation that they are already having in their mind. More about that later, but plant that seed in your mind.

Most think that if they run an advertisement in the newspaper, people will read it. That's not true. They will only read it if you capture their attention, promise them a benefit, and then give them a good reason to keep reading your ad.

It really takes a lot, a super-powerful reason, to get someone to divert their attention from reading the newspaper or magazine, to actually tearing out your ad so they can act on it later.

Marketing studies have proven that by changing as little as one word in the headline of an advertisement, the results of the ad can be increased by as much as seventeen times.

That's huge!

And most ads that I see in the newspaper are terrible. I mean terrible! It would be so easy to change just a few words in each of these ads and increase the response dramatically.

That's why I am writing this book, and why I am creating "Turn the Crank Marketing Mastermind Groups" around the country.

This is a lesson in leveraging your advertising dollars.

If you spend $500 on advertising, do you want those ads to bring in $300 worth of business, $500 worth of business, $1,000 worth of business, or $10,000 worth of business?

This is a legitimate question because you can increase the dollars coming in without increasing the cost of your advertising.

1. When I did the ad critique for my customer, one of the very first things that I noticed was a small photo in the bottom left corner of the ad. The photo was of really poor quality and you couldn't even make out what it was supposed to be. But more importantly, even if the photo was crystal clear, it delivered absolutely no advertising message. A photo in an advertisement has a very specific job to do. Don't put a photo in your ad just because you can.

    If you use a photo, it has to be so powerful that it will draw your *targeted prospect* into your ad. Notice that I highlighted "targeted prospect". Your ad should only speak to the specific person whom you are targeting. Everybody who reads the paper is not your prospect, and you are only fooling yourself if you think they are.

2. The next thing that I noticed was the amount of space devoted to "what, where, when and how to contact" was way too much. That space can be put to better use. If you get people to read your ad with a powerful headline, then use a powerful offer to keep them reading the ad, they'll read the fine print at the bottom on how to take advantage of the offer and find your place of business.

3. The ad that I was reviewing also had been adulterated by the graphic artist who laid out the ad. He or she had added leafy-looking designs in all four corners of the ad. Not only is this a gross waste of valuable space, but it makes the advertisement look like an "ad", and people are convinced that "they don't read ads". It also detracts from the powerful, attention-grabbing headline that I am about to suggest for this ad.

4. Now on to the heartbeat of the ad; the headline. After implementing all of the changes that I've already suggested, we have freed up a lot of space so the headline can be much, much larger. The headline is the most important part of the ad, so the bigger it is, the more likely it will be read. All advertisements need super-powerful headlines.

5. The offer in the ad I was reviewing was wishy-washy. A wishy-washy offer will convince people not to show up. This advertisement was for a plant sale, and this is how I read the offer:

"$6.50 plant sale! No wait, if I buy three they're only $6, but if I buy ten they're only $5, but I don't need ten! But I hate to pay $6.50 if I could have gotten them for $5. Maybe I'll wait, I'm not sure what to do."

Indecision has killed many a sale. Don't give people a reason to waffle. Give them a reason to take action immediately. Keep them focused on exactly what you want them to do.

I realize that by using the progressive price reduction strategy, my customer was trying to increase the number of plants that a person buys. But I think it confuses the reader and discourages them from coming to your sale. Your goal is to get them to tear the ad out of the paper, call a friend, and say, "Come on, let's go to this plant sale." The offer has to be powerful enough to get them to do that.

You really have to stop and study the dynamics of what it takes to get a person to respond to an advertisement, and what actions they take after they make that decision. You have to fully understand the power of successful advertisement and the leverage that a really powerful advertisement can give you once you get your prospective customers up off the couch.

6. So, let's re-do the headline. We'll change it to "Huge Plant Sale! 3,997 Plants Must be Sold at Just $4.97 Each!"

That's powerful. Every plant is only $4.97 and there are 3,997 of them to choose from. That will get them to the plant sale.

Did I really reduce the price from $6.50 to $4.97? No, I didn't because most people will buy at least three plants to get the reduced price, so very few people would have paid the $6.50 price anyway. You are looking for dozens of customers to show up in droves, create a buying frenzy and start grabbing plants like crazy.

Having experience with these types of plant sales, I can assure you, that's how it works.

7. So what's the difference between a $5 plant and a $4.97 plant?

   Two things. Three pennies, and a huge psychological difference! In a person's mind $4.97 sounds a lot lower than $5 even though the difference is only three pennies. Furthermore, one of the greatest marketers of all times tested prices constantly and concluded that any price ending in 7 out-pulled any other price point he used. $4.97 will out-pull $5 all day long.

Now back to the dynamics of getting a person to respond to your ad. Let's say that Mary sees your headline, reads your ad, and realizes that you have Japanese Red Maples for just $4.97. Mary is on a fixed income and very conservative, so she only wants that one plant. But she loves deals, and so does her daughter and her best friend Kathy. So she calls up both of them and invites them to come with her to the "huge plant sale".

Now Mary, who responds with the intent of only buying one plant, drags along her daughter and friend who may buy a lot more plants. Monday morning at work, Mary's daughter is going to tell her co-workers about all of the great deals she got at your plant sale. It's the Rule of 250 that we've already discussed.

Now, the only reason you got Mary to do this for you is because you let her buy just one plant at $4.97, and now she is a raving fan, telling the world about you.

Friends, it really does work this way. Don't chase away those one-plant-buying customers. They are valuable.

Back to my initial comments about changing just one word in a headline and increasing the results by as much as seventeen times. I suggested a minimum of seven different changes to this ad. I firmly believe that the changes I suggested will change the response dramatically.

The most important change being a big bold headline that screams "$4.97 plants must be sold!" But when you add that to all of the more subtle changes I suggested, this ad becomes a powerful business-building machine.

It's all about leveraging your advertising dollars!

One thing I forgot to mention. With an offer like this I don't like giving people too much contact information. What we are advertising here is an event. You cannot experience an event by asking questions over the phone. So I do everything I can to make people get in the car and drive out to experience it for themselves. More people will show up, and they will buy. They might even come back the next day or next weekend. They'll probably even talk about your plant sale the next day at work.

With all of that said, below is the ad that I would run. It's the same size and the same cost to run as the ad that I reviewed, but it will grab at least ten times more attention, and ten times as many people will show up.

Which ad do you think will jump off the page as your
prospective customers skim their daily newspaper?
Which do you think will result in a better return on
investment? I know which one will work better, for all of
the reasons described above.

You really need to give this "leverage your advertising
dollars" thing some serious attention. The daily
newspapers are filled with advertisements that are
performing at ten percent of their potential. That's why
you don't see them repeated often enough.

Most business owners have a perverted understanding
of what advertising is supposed to do.

Advertising is supposed to make you money.
Immediately.
Not three weeks from now, three months from now, or three years from now.

Advertising sales reps will *erroneously* tell you that your prospective customers need to see your ad seven or nine times before they take action. I'm sorry, but that's just a bunch of crap to get you to run an unsuccessful advertisement over and over for their personal financial gain.

Every dollar you spend on advertising should *immediately* bring you a return on your investment.

Done correctly, you never have to use your own money to pay for advertising because you buy it on credit, and before the bill comes in the mail you've already deposited the money it's made for you in the bank.

At the time of this writing, I currently have an advertising campaign that runs from $3,000 to $8,000 a month. I started this campaign with a budget of $1,500 a month, and that was years ago. It was charged to my credit card, and I've never used one dime of my own money on these ads. Nor have I paid a dime in interest on this money. The ads always bring in enough money to pay the advertising bill long before the bill comes in the mail.

As I just stated, I started my advertising campaign years ago as a test. After a few days I knew it was working and profitable, so I've been increasing the amounts ever since.

My ads are "vending machine predictable", running constantly while I sleep, work and play. The only thing that I do is pay the bill when my credit card statement arrives in the mail.

My ads appear, prospective customers see my ads, respond, and give me money. It doesn't get any better than that.

How to Write Advertising Copy That Works

If there is one thing that small business owners do consistently which cripples the effectiveness of their marketing, it would be writing or creating really poor advertisements or other marketing pieces.

Most business owners don't just do this poorly, they are horrendous at it. And to make matters worse, they *really think they are good at it!!!*

They are not good at it. Their advertisements are absolutely terrible and the newspapers, trade magazines and yellow pages are full of terrible ads.

Which side of this fence do you want to be on?

Do you want your ego to stand in the way of your business becoming super successful? Or are you willing to say, "Maybe McGroarty is right. Maybe my ads aren't so good after all. Maybe I need to *really* learn how to write *powerful and super-effective* advertising copy."

(Hint) Learning how to write super-effective advertising copy is one of the most important skills you can learn in your lifetime.

I am going to show you a formula for writing powerful, super-effective ad copy. This formula should be applied to any advertising you do; newspaper, yellow pages, trade magazines, direct-mail letters, radio and television spots.

It doesn't matter what you sell, the formula still applies. Your business is not different and your potential customers are not different. This is the formula you should use to sell ice cream cones, small plants, legal services, hydraulic valves, jet engines or space shuttles.

This is not some lamebrained idea that I've come up with on my own. I've studied the best advertising copywriters this world has known, and this is the condensed version of what I've learned in 22 years of studying these brilliant marketers.

One of the people whom I've studied intensely was the late Gary Halbert, and I once heard Gary say something that has stayed with me all these years because I know it's true. This is a quote: "You are one sales letter away from making more money than you can sensibly spend in a life-time."

In other words, all you need is one good letter and you just keep mailing that letter over and over and over until it quits working. A letter that is "vending machine predictable".

Okay, let's get started. This lesson is the most important part of this book. Learn it well and prosper.

The most important part of an advertisement is the headline. All ads, all sales letters, any and all advertising that you do should have a powerful headline. Think about how you read the newspaper. You open the paper and scan the page, glancing at the headlines, and from there you decide what articles you are going to read.

You're busy, I'm busy, everybody is busy. We all try to stay informed and read the newspaper and magazines that interest us, but there is no way that we can read the entire publications, and in most cases we actually only read a small percentage of what appears in these publications.

The only criteria we use to determine what we read and what we don't read are the headlines. Yes, there are other things besides headlines that catch our attention in the newspaper, but for the most part we have trained ourselves to read headlines. If a photo catches your eye, what do you do? You read the caption under the photo. So if you have a photo in your ad, by all means put a caption under it that is written in the best headline style that you can muster.

Should you have a photo in your ad? That depends, and I'll get to that in a bit. For right now, let's concentrate on headlines. Headlines fall into just a few categories:

News
Self-interest
Curiosity
Humor

Humor is a dangerous game to play and I never use humor in a headline. People have different senses of humor and a humor headline can either not work at all because your prospective customer did not get the joke, or they can backfire horribly because they are misinterpreted. Ad space is expensive. Stick with something that is going to pull like a magnet.

Curiosity can work, but the curious headline must contain some key words that are mental or emotional triggers to the reader. One of the greatest headlines of all times was used to sell music lessons via mail order. This particular headline outperformed dozens and dozens of other headlines that were also tested in this ad, and the "They all laughed" headline ran for years and years. This is the complete headline:

"They all laughed when I sat down at the piano . . . but when I started to play . . ."

This headline is curious, but it also contains several emotional triggers. First of all, it refers to playing the piano. A lot of people who cannot play the piano would love to be able to play, so the word *piano* is actually an emotional trigger for those who secretly wish they could play the piano.

But the phrase "they all laughed" is a huge emotional trigger. At one time or another, we have all experienced people laughing at us, and to think just for a second that we could suddenly turn that around and have them laughing at themselves for laughing at us, is a huge emotional trigger.

Even though those kinds of emotion-provoking headlines can be super effective, you usually don't have to go that deep to create an effective headline. That's why news and self-interest headlines are so effective.

A news headline is one that announces something new, something that will get peoples' attention.

Mary's Café Now Serves Ice Cream

The above headline is a news type of headline, but it's a bit dangerous because it assumes the reader is already familiar with Mary's Café. Something like this . . .

New Arthritis Treatment is So Effective You'll Feel 20 Years Younger

is much better because it contains a huge emotional trigger, the word *arthritis*, and it indicates that there is something new on the market which promises a better quality of life.

Trust me, a headline like that will stop an arthritis sufferer in their tracks as they are scanning their daily newspaper. And that's what a headline should do.

A headline has two jobs. One is to stop the reader in their tracks and hold their attention for just a few seconds. The second is to draw them into the rest of the ad by promising a benefit. Once the reader realizes that they somehow might benefit, they slip out of scanning-the-page mode, into a more relaxed, more attentive, learning or discovery mode. From there they are drawn into the well written advertising copy that will capture and hold their attention. In other words, they are on the slippery slope.

Mail order genius Joe Sugarman teaches that an advertisement is like a slippery slope with the top of the advertisement being the top of the slope, and once your prospect steps on that slippery slope, they will slide down into your ad, all the way through your ad, on down to the call for action, which is the part of the ad where you tell your prospect exactly what to do. In example:

"Call now!"

"Order right now!"

"Clip this ad and bring it in today."

"Grab Mama and get in the car, drive out right now."

Every advertisement that you create, be it a newspaper ad, magazine ad, web page, radio or TV spot, should have a well structured format that looks something like this:

  A powerful headline
  One or more powerful sub-headlines
  Captivating body copy
  A strong call to action
  Contact information

All super-effective advertisements are crafted exactly as I've just described. The key word here is *crafted*. All really effective advertisements are methodically crafted. They are not thrown together at the last minute as the ad rep stands over your shoulder saying, "Oh yes, that's very nice." Sometimes it takes days, weeks, or even months of tweaking before your advertisement is capable of running at full speed.

As a matter of fact, when you give your advertisement to the ad rep, he or she will likely look at you kind of funny because they have no idea what a good advertisement looks like, and they'll try to talk you into changing the ad so it looks like all of the other ads in the publication. Don't fall for it. Stick to your guns and follow the formula that you are learning here.

This stuff really, really works.

Pay close attention to what you just read about how people skim through a publication reading headlines, in seconds deciding what articles they will read and what articles they won't read. That's why it is so important that your advertisements have strong, attention-grabbing headlines which promise the reader a benefit.

The headline is the advertisement for the ad, so if the headline fails to capture the reader's attention and arouse their interest, the rest of the ad, no matter how good it is, will never be seen.

For months now I have been procrastinating about calling someone to clean our carpets. I don't know who I want to call so I need to shop for a carpet cleaner, something that I have no time for.

Just a few days ago I was reading the paper, really just skimming the paper as I just described. Since I've been working on this book for several months now, my subconscious mind is very attune to any and all advertising that I see in a day, and I couldn't help but notice the dozens and dozens of really poorly crafted ads that appear in the newspaper each day.

While looking at these poorly done advertisements, mentally changing each one, (it's a habit that I have) knowing that these subtle changes would dramatically increase response, I came across a poorly done ad for a carpet cleaner. Even though the ad was poorly done, I picked up the phone and gave them a call. I learned a little about the company, then scheduled carpet cleaning. About $325 worth of work.

But here's my point . . .

Of the 60,000 people who received that newspaper that day, how many of those people have also been procrastinating about calling a carpet cleaner? How many of them noticed the ad? I'll answer the question for you since I know the answer.

Exactly ten percent of those who should have seen the ad!

I don't know the exact number, but I do know that if the ad had been crafted with a well written headline which demanded attention and promised a benefit, it would have pulled ten times more response than it did.

And with that said, do you realize how many more times they could run that ad each week? Knowing a little about our local paper and their ad rates, I'd say the cost of the ad was around $275. Let's say it brought in three jobs with an average sale of $200 per job, which is probably average for carpet cleaning.

That's $600 from a $275 ad.

Is that good?

No, it's not good! That means that 45 percent of every dollar went to advertising cost.

But what if the ad was better crafted and pulled in twenty jobs at $200 each?

That's $4,000, which really is very realistic from a well crafted and well written advertisement. In this scenario you would only be giving up seven percent of your revenue to advertising costs. That means you get to keep $93 of every $100 that you earn!

That's what I mean by leveraging your advertising dollars. The cost of the ad doesn't change, but by just changing the words on the paper, the advertisement can easily bring in ten times more money.

And if you had an advertisement or a sales letter that could do that, you would be crazy not to run it continuously, constantly bringing you a steady stream of new customers.

It would be "vending machine predictable".

Now back to crafting a powerful and effective advertisement. We've established that all advertisements need a super powerful, attention-grabbing, benefit-promising headline that will stop people in their tracks and draw them into your advertisement.

All advertisements should also have one or more powerful sub-headlines. A sub-headline is just a second or third headline that is strategically placed in the body copy of the advertisement. It's still set in a bold typeface, but in a smaller font than the primary headline.

The reason you need sub-headlines is to further draw prospects into your ad. Let's say that your primary headline grabbed your prospects' attention and slowed them down enough to at least give your advertisement a second look, but as of yet they have not committed themselves to read your ad.

One or more well crafted, super powerful sub-headlines will do the trick and pull them into the advertisement to the point that they read every single word in the ad.

It's essential that you understand the psychology of what is happening in the subconscious mind of the prospects you are trying to reach. They don't want to read your ad. They like to think and tell others that they never read the ads in the newspaper or magazines that they read. So deep down inside they are quite resistant to reading your ad. They are doing everything possible, *not to read your advertisement!*

That's a huge hurdle to overcome.

That's why really good advertisements are crafted in such a way that you tap into a different part of the prospect's subconscious mind. You have to find the emotional trigger that is more powerful than their built-in resistance to reading advertisements.

When a prospect is reading their daily newspaper or magazine, their eyes scan each page looking for articles and maybe advertisements that interest them. When your super-effective headline grabs their attention, they are not immediately committed to reading your ad. Instead, they simply give it a second look, scanning over the ad quickly, subconsciously looking for something or anything that might interest them. So after quickly reading your headline, the next thing they'll do is read any sub-headlines that are in the advertisement, and maybe read the caption under the photo, if there is a photo in your advertisement.

The body copy of your advertisement is the meat and potatoes of your ad. The body copy is the workhorse that gets the job done. That's where you tell your compelling story, and tell it in such a way that the prospect is compelled to take immediate action.

So with that in mind, every other element in your advertisement has to be critically and intentionally designed to get that prospect hooked and back to the top of the ad. Then you can draw them into the ad and into the body copy where you can tell your compelling story. Each element in the ad has a specific job to do.

The job of the headline is to grab the prospect's attention and draw them into the ad, getting them to read the sub-headlines and eventually the body copy that will take them right down to the call for action.

Sub-headlines should be designed to further arouse the interest of the prospect, promise them more benefits, and take them back to the top of the ad where they can begin their journey through the advertisement.

Keep in mind, once you get their attention, promise them a benefit in the headline, then more benefits in the sub-headlines, you will then have their undivided attention and they will read the rest of your advertisement with great interest.

The ultimate goal of each element in the advertisement is to get them to read the body copy. If you use a photo in your ad, it should only be there if it will give the prospect a powerful reason to read the rest of the ad.

For instance, let's say that you sell patio enclosures. Putting a photo of the owner of the company in an ad does nothing for the prospect and gives them no compelling reason to read the ad. Including a photo of all of your trucks lined up in a row also means nothing to the prospect. "So what! You've got a lot of trucks."

But include a photo of a beautiful patio enclosure that shows the homeowners comfortably relaxing in their patio enclosure, with a caption that reads,

> "This beautiful patio room only
> took three days to complete."

Now you have my attention if I have been subconsciously thinking about getting estimates on a patio room. That photo will draw me back to the top of the ad, and if the headline and sub-headlines are well crafted and promise me a benefit, I am going to read the rest of the advertisement and likely pick up the phone and call.

So each and every element in the advertisement must be intentionally crafted to pull the prospect into the ad where they can read the body copy and "experience" your compelling story.

Now let's discuss body copy. Body copy is the actual written story within the advertisement. Most advertisements that you see have little or no body copy at all, and this is a huge mistake that makes these ads weak and only fractionally effective. Body copy is the place in your ad where you tell your story. People love stories, and they do read them. Go back and reread my ad for Pinky's Hamburger Joint, and reread the ad I used for our final year of plant sales. Both of those ads tell brief but compelling stories.

Most small business owners think that too many words in an advertisement will keep people from reading the ad. If that's what you think, you are wrong. Keep in mind, a well crafted advertisement has a powerful headline and powerful sub-headlines that leave the reader asking for more information.

You have their attention, you've aroused their interest and now you must finish telling your story, and tell it in such a way that you will hold their interest and build their desire for the product that you are selling. In other words, close the sale. They have a strong interest or they wouldn't be this deep into your ad.

So how do you take them from an interested prospect to a buying customer?

This part is actually really easy if you just grasp these concepts and put a great deal of thought and effort into your advertisement. Remember, an advertisement is not something that you throw together at the last minute, or worse yet, delegate to somebody else in your company.

You craft an advertisement with a great deal of thought and effort, keeping in mind that once you get it perfect, or near perfect, you can use it over and over for many years to come.

You get into the head of your prospective customer and you figure out exactly what they are thinking.

What problem do they have in their life that you or your product can solve?

Now comes the psychology, and if you don't use psychology in your advertising you are cheating yourself out of tens of thousands of dollars in profit.

Inside all of us there are secret, or not so secret wants, desires and cravings. And I do mean all of us. In order to be an effective advertiser you must truly understand what these wants, desires and cravings are, and discover how to leverage them as you craft your ads.

Once you get the hang of this, you truly will be in control of your own destiny. You will no longer be victim to unpredictable changes in your universe. You will be able to manipulate the universe around you, and others will never be able to completely figure out why things are going so well for you and not for them.

You have to trust me on this, but this truly is powerful stuff.

Okay, let's get into it.

First of all, examine this sentence again:

"Inside all of us there are secret, or not so secret wants, desires and cravings."

Notice that the word *need* does not appear in that sentence? Remember this old adage? "Find a need and fill it if you want to succeed in business."

It's not true.

People don't buy what they need.

They buy what they want, desire and crave!

In order for you to craft an effective advertisement or sales letter, you have to really understand your prospective customer. You have to get into their head and figure out what they want, desire and crave.

Time out.

If you sell business to business, you might be thinking that this does not apply to you because business-to-business marketing is devoid of emotion. If that's what you think, you are wrong, and we'll get more in depth about business-to-business marketing later in this book.

Below is a short list of some of the most powerful emotions which drive the purchasing decisions that people make.

There was a time when you could create a list for women and a list for men. But with so many women working full time, and many of them very career oriented, and more and more men doing the stay-at-home-dad thing, those lines are blurred and many of the things on this list are now interchangeable. Not all, but many.

People want to be, in no particular order:

Successful
Happy
Rich
Envied
Loved
Recognized
Thin
Physically fit
Famous
Emotionally secure
Financially secure
Popular
Admired
Attractive
Sexy
Sexually desired
Considered an authority or an expert

People want to have:

Nice cars
Nice homes
Money
More friends
Great jobs
Successful careers
Expensive toys
Satisfying relationships
Anything that will make others envious

In a nutshell that's pretty much it. Some advertising copywriters consider the list to be much shorter, claiming that the list can be narrowed down to money, sex and greed. And if you look at the lists again, each item on the lists really does fall into one of those three categories.

Another super-successful copywriter whom I've studied extensively says that people buy for these three reasons: greed, greed and greed. Look at the lists again. He's pretty close.

So now you have to figure out exactly which of these emotional appeals is the most prevalent in the mind of your prospect. In order to effectively do that, you have to really get to know your prospective customers inside and out.

How do you do that?

By studying the buying and personal habits of your existing customers. The customers that you are currently doing business with and those you have done business with in the past have many things in common. It could be age, gender, income, area of residence, social status or other demographic markers that you can identify.

In other words, not everyone in town or across the country is your prospect. You have to narrow your focus to only *those who are predisposed to do business with you.*

If you sell medium- to high-priced riding lawnmowers in your local community, you start narrowing your focus by eliminating apartment dwellers and condominium owners. Then you can further narrow your focus by eliminating people whose annual income makes them unlikely candidates for your lawnmowers since that demographic group typically opts for a much less expensive brand.

What about women? Do women buy your lawnmowers?

I'm sure some do, but if 95 percent of your sales are to men, then you should target your marketing exclusively to that 95-percentile group. That doesn't mean you won't sell to women, and you certainly don't want to offend anybody, but by the same token you must stay focused and not get all namby-pamby trying to please everybody on the street.

Your marketing must be narrowly focused to your target market. Then if others respond to your marketing, that's fine, and from that you might discover another niche market you can target.

For instance, just for a moment let's think about the women who have purchased your lawnmowers, that five-percentile group that we eliminated just a moment ago.

What is it about them that makes them unique? How can they be identified? What kind of vehicle do they drive? A pickup truck? Where do they live? What hobbies do they have? Do they own horses? Something. If you look at each one demographically you might find an overlooked and unexploited target market that you can tap.

Do you see where I'm going with this line of questioning? You should also ask the same questions about the men, the 95-percentile group. It's really important that you don't just "accept any customer who comes in the door", but study those customers so you know where to find more just like them. Then create marketing that is targeted to that specific group. It's really important to be able to picture your ideal customer in your mind as you craft your advertising piece. When you are done, the marketing piece will speak directly to the group you are targeting, and it will speak to them in the language they are most familiar with. All demographic groups have a language all their own, along with certain slang terms that might belong in your advertising piece as well.

This is all part of getting into the head of your prospective customers. In order to do this effectively, you have to learn enough about your prospective customer that you can become that person as you are crafting the advertising piece. Then you can effectively use emotional triggers that will really resonate with the person you are targeting.

Not too long ago, I was consulting with a guy who had a karate school, and he was having problems getting enough kids into his after-school programs which were really aimed at younger children. Instead of sending your child to daycare after school, he would pick them up at school and transport them to his karate school where he would help them build self esteem and other strong social skills, as well as a little self defense.

What he was failing to capitalize on is the guilt that working moms have about sending their kids to daycare. I showed him how to take this negative emotion of daycare and turning it into a positive emotion because their child would actually have fun and learn valuable skills at his karate school.

So in essence, he had to mentally become a working mom to fully understand the emotions she was going through in making the decision to send her child to daycare.

An advertising copywriter of long ago by the name of Robert Collier taught us that "you have to join the conversation that your prospect is already having with themselves in order to effectively sell them your product or service".

Read that quote over and over until you have it committed to memory and you truly understand what it means.

In my twenty-two years of studying and writing powerful advertising copy, I cling to that one sentence more than anything else I've learned.

Whether you are crafting a newspaper, yellow pages or magazine advertisement, writing a radio commercial, a direct-mail sales letter, a handout flyer or a business card, all you have to do is follow these simple steps and apply the psychology that you just learned.

1. Write a powerful headline that attracts the attention of people who will be inclined to buy what you are selling.

2. In that headline, promise them a benefit so powerful that they have no choice, they must give it their attention.

3. Write one or more powerful sub-headlines that will leave them craving more information about your powerful offer.

4. Keep in mind that the headline and the sub-headlines must join the conversation that your prospect is already having with themselves. In example;

   "I have to hire somebody to clean this carpet."

   "I must find a new auto mechanic. Somebody who's honest and reasonable."

   "We need a supplier of fasteners that actually delivers on time!"

   "It's our anniversary. Where can I take her that's really special?"

   The above examples are actual, everyday conversations that people have with themselves. No matter what you sell, your prospects are having similar conversations with themselves.

   Join them!

5. Use powerful body copy in your advertisements. Tell a compelling story that builds interest, then desire for your product or service. Mentally become your prospective customer and write the story from their perspective. Convince them that you can solve their problem.

6. Ask for the order. Tell them exactly what you want them to do right now. *"Pick up the phone*

and call right now!" If your phones are not answered 24 hours a day, give them a website they can visit at any time from which they can order.

7. Make sure every element - photos, captions or graphics - in the advertisement makes them more curious and leads them to the top of ad. Make sure they read your advertisement in the sequential order that *you* want them to follow.

Hello?
Hello?
Hello?

About the website. If you put a website in your advertisement, it must be a mirror image of the advertisement or sales letter that sent them there, only better, with more details, more compelling photos and audio testimonials.

Do not send them to your generic website designed by your local internet geek!

The website that you send them to should be written and laid out using the exact formula I just laid out for you. But with a website you can do much, much more. You can have audio testimonials, more photos, color photos, streaming video and so on.

You can also capture their name and email address *with their permission to email them anytime you like!*

That's huge.

But be careful. Don't send them to a website if what you really want them to do is to call right now. Don't give them room or time to waffle. If it's in your best interest to sell them right now, on the spot, then that's what you should do.

Keep in mind, if you send them to a website only a small percentage will actually join your email list. These days people guard their email address with their life. They don't want more spam.

Don't assume that every person who lands on your webpage is going to join your email list. That is completely not the case. In order to get an email address from a prospect, you have to work really hard at it and give them free bonuses and all kinds of things before they'll give up their email address.

Getting an email address is an art unto itself.

But I'm good at it.

At the time of this writing I've got 137,000 people on my email list. Those are people who have added themselves to my list one at a time, and have given me permission to email them any time I choose.

Our local newspaper that serves the better part of three counties only has about 65,000 subscribers. I've got twice that many on my email list. And when I write to them, which is usually about once a week, they give me money. Thousands of dollars each time I mail the list.

It's a handy little tool to have, but that's a topic for another time.

Color Versus Black and White, and Ad Placement

Today many newspapers are offering to run your advertisement in color. Is that a good idea, or a bad idea?

It depends on any number of things, and only true scientific testing would tell you for sure. With a true A/B split test you would know for sure, but that's tricky and you'd have to get the newspaper to cooperate.

So this is my take. I like black and white ads, and this is why. First of all, we already discussed what the mindset is of the newspaper-reading public. They claim to not read the ads, only the articles. For all of their adult lives they have trained themselves to skim the newspaper, briefly glancing over the headlines, deciding what to read and what not to read.

So they have trained themselves to look at anything that looks like an article and has a black and white headline.

So a full color ad in the middle of the page screams "Advertisement!"

Now if the ad was done correctly, and was actually placed right smack in the middle of the page, I might think differently, but that's not likely to happen. Newspapers tend to group all of the color ads in one spot.

Therefore, the entire group of ads screams, "Advertisements!"

So for now I remain convinced that black and white ads, properly written and laid out, will give you a much higher return on investment.

But what about ad placement?

This is where you have to kick and fight to get your ad placed where you want it to appear in the newspaper. So where do you want it to appear?

Forget about how you read the newspaper. You are not your own prospect. Yeah, yeah, I know. You are going to argue with me on this one, but do so at your own financial loss.

The absolutely best place for your advertisement is in the first part of the newspaper, the main news section.

Everybody reads the main news section.

And from there throughout the rest of the newspaper, readership drops off. This is a fact. Don't listen to sales representatives from the newspaper, they have no idea what they are talking about. Last week they were working at Wendy's and next week they will be selling cars. Take no advice from them.

The ideal place for your advertisement would be right smack in the middle of page three, just above the fold. But that's probably not going to happen, so the best you can do is kick and fight for the main news section, then when it doesn't appear there, call the advertising manager and whine like a baby. Tell him or her that you wasted the grocery money because of poor placement.

Maybe you'll get your way. It's worked for me. It's well worth the fight because good placement can improve your results dramatically.

Advertise a Compelling Offer!

This is very, very important. Remember what you've already learned about leveraging your advertising dollars? The best way to leverage those advertising dollars and get absolutely the most return on investment is to do advertising that makes a powerful offer, that your *targeted prospects* will have a difficult time ignoring.

Remember the ad that I ran for years selling re-landscaping services? Those ads made a compelling offer. They promised an attractive price, then the ad went on to describe exactly what services we were going to perform for that amount of money. The ad went on to explain that the price included topsoil, mulch, and an assortment of plants. The only thing that the ads did not do was quantify the amount of materials because they did vary from home to home.

But it was an offer that was so powerful, any person who fit my customer profile could not pass it up. They at least had to call to investigate the offer further.

The offer was powerful and it worked so well that the very first ad pulled at 33.3 times ad cost and the later ads, after I raised the price and had to switch to different media, pulled at twenty times ad cost.

It was the offer. That's why those ads worked.

My $4.97 plant sale ads pulled between twenty and twenty-eight times ad cost because of the offer.

Now let's switch gears and look at a completely different type of business. We'll use the auto repair shop business in this example.

First of all, what do we know about the auto repair shop business?

It can be competitive. Everybody has a car or two or three. Not all customers are equal. Some customers can barely afford gas for their car, but when it breaks down they still need to get it repaired. But oftentimes they can't pick it up for days until they can find the money to pay for the repairs.

But we also know that the very best customers have a really high lifetime customer value. In other words, once you have a really good customer who can afford to repair everything on their car that needs to be repaired, they will stay with you as a customer for a very long time. Providing you take really good care of them.

Remember what you discovered about the lifetime value of a customer?

Okay, as an auto repair shop owner we need to advertise to get more customers. And we know that we must make a really compelling offer in order to get the best return on investment of our advertising dollars. What are our options?

We can run a namby-pamby ad that says something like...

Joe's Garage

We're the best in town. We service all makes and models, and we accept all major credit cards. $5 off your first oil change with this ad. First time customers only.

Will this ad work? Maybe, but not very well. What about this ad?

Free Oil Change!

This is not a gimmick. We are doing Free oil changes! Just bring in this ad and we'll change your oil and filter, rotate your tires and perform a free brake inspection. This free offer also includes a free grease job, and we'll even lubricate your door hinges, check all the lights, and top off your windshield washer fluid and check the air in your tires. Oh well, I might as well throw in a free exterior car wash while I'm in such a generous mood. I'm not kidding, all of these things are free, just bring in this ad. Or just stop in and say, "Hey Joe, I want a free oil change".

**Joe's Garage 000-0000
1234 Main St.
This offer expires 1/1/09**

Now that's a compelling offer, but I know what you're thinking. *"That's the craziest idea I've ever seen."*

Maybe. Maybe not.

If you were an auto repair shop owner and you ran that ad in the local newspaper, do you think it would work? Of course it would. You'd be buried in new business! You'd have cars lined up out the door, into the street and down the road as far as you could see.

Again, I know what you're thinking; *"Yeah, and by the end of the week I'd be dead and bankrupt!"* Maybe, but you have to admit, it is an extremely powerful offer!

So . . . maybe we're on to something.

You're right, making this incredibly attractive offer to the general public would be a little on the crazy side, because the one thing it would do for sure is bring out all of the bottom feeders.

It's not a very attractive term, but "bottom feeders" are that class of the population who are in search of every deal, every coupon, every buy-one-get-one-free offer they can find. They jump from merchant to merchant every time they can save a few pennies.

So even though they will respond to extremely attractive offers, they really have poor lifetime customer value. Those are not the customers you are looking for, no matter what business you're in.

Okay, so we've concluded that the "free oil change" offer would work, but it would also attract a lot of customers who don't really fit our ideal customer profile if we were to run it as an advertisement in our local newspaper.

Here's the answer. This is how any auto repair shop can and should attract new customers who fit their ideal customer profile.

Let's say that the ideal customer for an auto repair shop is one who lives in a house that has a household income of $125,000 per year or more. It's safe to say that most of the people in this income bracket own at least two, if not three or four cars. One or two of those cars might be new and covered under a warranty, but the other cars are most likely not. They probably have kids in high school or college who are driving cars with high mileage, cars that need mechanical work on a regular basis. They very well could have hobby cars, maybe an old Mustang or Corvette.

It's also safe to say that people in that income bracket don't do their own auto repairs. It's also a sure bet that they have a high lifetime customer value. Once they find an auto repair shop they really like, they will come back often *and they will refer others!*

That "refer others" is huge. Don't overlook it.

When you combine their lifetime customer value with their likelihood to refer others, they become very attractive prospects for any auto repair shop. So . . . how do you reach customers like that, and how do you get them to come into your shop for the first time?

You implement the small business vending machine strategy and you let it run unabated on a till forbid basis. In other words, you set up your marketing plan, you put it in motion, and you make it perpetual so it just keeps happening over and over until you stop it.

Implementing the Small Business Vending Machine Strategy and Letting It Run Unabated On a "Till Forbid" Basis

Pay attention folks, this is the genius of this system.

This is your goal: Get prospective customers who live in your market, who have a household income of $125,000 per year or more, into your shop for the first time.

This is how you do it:

You find a printshop/mailing shop that can print letters and coupons for you, but you also need a company that can do the mailings for you. Just look in your local yellow pages, there should be a number of them you can choose from, and they don't even have to be local to you.

You'll ask them to create two things for you. One is a coupon that contains this advertisement:

Free Oil Change!

This is not a gimmick. We are doing Free oil changes! Just bring in this ad and we'll change your oil and filter, rotate your tires and perform a free brake inspection. This free offer also includes a free grease job, and we'll even lubricate your door hinges, check all the lights, and top off your windshield washer fluid and check the air in your tires. Oh well, I might as well throw in a free exterior car wash while I'm in such a generous mood. I'm not kidding, all of these things are free, just bring in this ad. Or just stop in and say, "Hey Joe, I want a free oil change". –Joe

Joe's Garage 000-0000
1234 Main St.
This offer expires 1/1/09

Have them make it look nice with a certificate-type border around it, and have them print it on cardstock, not regular 20-lb. paper.

You will also have them print this letter for you:

Joe's Garage
1234 Main St.
Your Town, State 00000

Free Oil Change!

Dear Friend,

My name is Joe Mechanic and I've got an auto repair shop over here on Main St. You may not know me, and that's exactly why I would like to give you a free oil change. I'd like to get to know you, and I'd like for you to try our services just once and get to know me.

The easiest way to do that is to give you a FREE oil change. No gimmicks, no strings attached, nothing like that. I know that if you try our service just once, you are likely to come back when you need another oil change or a car repair.

Sure, I'll lose money on the FREE oil change, but if you become a regular, satisfied customer it's worth it for both of us.

I'm sincere about this, I'd really like to meet you, and I'd like you to get to know us and experience why our shop is different.

Just call for an appointment and mention this letter or the enclosed gift card and we'll change your oil and filter, rotate your tires and perform a free brake inspection.

This free offer also includes a free grease job, and we'll even lubricate your door hinges, check all the lights, and top off your windshield washer fluid and check the air in your tires. And you'll also get a free exterior car wash.

I look forward to meeting you.

Sincerely,

Joe Mechanic

PS: If you are already one of our customers, then I'd like to say thank you for being a customer, and please, by all means call for an appointment to take advantage of this FREE offer.

I don't care what kind of business you are in, this strategy is powerful, and it will work over and over and over for years.

Points to consider:

1. It makes a very powerful offer that few people could ignore. The offer is believable because we've used a strategy known as "reason why". "Reason why" advertising copy explains why you are making the offer so people don't suspect a scam.
2. It targets the ideal prospect with pinpoint accuracy.
3. It targets prospects who have really high lifetime value.
4. It targets prospects who have the potential to refer other customers with really high lifetime value.
5. Running this same offer over and over will eventually allow you to fire some customers who don't fall into your ideal-customer profile.
6. The letter should be hand signed in blue ink, or printed in two colors with only the signature appearing in blue ink to make it appear to be

signed by hand. This letter is very important. It's the first contact with people who you intend to do business with forever. Take the time to hand sign them, or have them printed as described.

7. You can pick any number of neighborhoods surrounding your business and mail this letter to them over and over for years. Keep in mind, giving an existing customer a free oil change is just plain smart business. They will reciprocate by giving you more business and sending you more referrals. This is known as the law of reciprocity. It works.

8. This letter and coupon are perfect vehicles to implement your "vending machine predictable" marketing campaign.

Keep in mind, the secret to this strategy is that only people who have a household income of $125,000 or more will receive these letters.

$125,000 in household income is just a number I used. Maybe you'd prefer people with a household income of $60,000 or $80,000. Do test mailings until you find the magic number.

Your printer/letter shop can easily specify the criteria that you are aiming for by address, zip code, household income, or even make-of-car if that's what you prefer.

Okay, now let's play devil's advocate. Let's say you launch this marketing strategy and it doesn't work. You don't get any calls, or all the wrong people come in. What do you do?

You find out why!

If a marketing campaign does not work, there is a reason. All you have to do is identify why it didn't work, fix the problem and go at it again.

If it fails to work, it is not because your business is different. You might have to tweak it a little for your business, but it will work, and you can take that to the bank.

Think about this campaign and then your own business. The power of this offer is "who do you want to do business with". Remember, that's where we started. We targeted people with a household income of $125,000 or more who live within a certain zip code range of your business.

"Who do you want to do business with" is the most important part of any marketing campaign you want to launch. You must identify your ideal prospect and market only to them.

"Yeah, but I also get a lot of other people into my shop."

Of course you do, and you always will. But that doesn't mean you want to market to "a lot of other people". You want to spend all of your marketing dollars targeting your ideal prospect.

This strategy alone will increase your profits dramatically.

Delegate It and Be Firm!

So . . . what's going to stop you from implementing a strategy like this one? Procrastination and your failure to delegate the responsibility to someone who will see it through.

I've been guilty of this so many times in my business life I don't even like to think about what this has cost me. But I can assure you, it's not tens of thousands of dollars. It's hundreds of thousands of dollars. How stupid of me!

So here's the deal. There are several different ways to manage a campaign like this. You can hire a printer and a mailing shop, or you can do a lot of it manually. Doing it manually is more difficult, but it does allow you to control how many pieces are mailed each day and so on.

As I write this, my twenty-year-old son who is home from college for the summer just launched a similar campaign for his summer landscaping business, and this is what I had him do.

First he wrote the letter. It was terrible so I rewrote it for him. Then I got a local street atlas and showed him in what neighborhoods I thought his letter would be the most successful.

Then I took him to the library and showed him how to use a Haines Criss Cross Directory. From the map we got the street names that he wanted to target, then from the Criss Cross Directory we got the names and addresses of the people on those streets and he is mailing his letters to those people.

The Haines Directory has a handy little feature that helps target the best residential neighborhoods. It's called a wealth index rating, and before each street in the directory they tell you what the wealth rating is. So really all you have to do is pick one street that you feel you know what kind of an income bracket they might be in, see what the wealth rating is, then pick other streets in your market with the same wealth rating.

Delegate it and be firm!
Delegate it and be firm!
Delegate it and be firm!

This is so, so important. This is not a job that you should be doing yourself. Your time is too valuable, you're too busy, and you hate this kind of work.

This may not be something that you give to your spouse to do. Spouses often get distracted, or they become judgmental and decide it's a waste of time because "we have enough business", or "we just need to blah, blah, blah."

Give this job to somebody in your organization and hold them accountable for getting X number of letters out each day! Or get somebody who's looking for something easy to do from home and let them do it.

You can also rent a list of names and addresses from a list broker. These days you either download them or they send them to you on a CD, and they usually offer you the chance to use them over and over if you pay a little extra for the list.

Keep in mind, I'm pretty sure the folks from Haines tell you right in the front of the directory that you are not allowed to take info from the directory and save it to a database. Make sure you read the rules!

No matter how you do it, this strategy works and can build your business at a fast rate if you actually use it without fail.

These Strategies Will Work for *Your Business!*

What you are learning here can be applied to any business, and it can be applied effectively. You just have to think it through. Let's start with a few simple questions:

1. Who are your ideal prospects?

2. What is it that sets them apart and makes them identifiable among the general population?

3. How can you reach them?

4. What problems do they have that you can solve?

5. What keeps them up at night?

6. What is the most effective way to reach them?

Answer these questions!

That's all you need to know. Once you honestly and effectively answer these six questions, you can proceed with a marketing plan that will be "vending machine predictable".

Let's say you own a company that makes really large, very expensive machines that take flat pieces of steel and bends those pieces of steel into U-shaped channels used in a variety of different industries.

Do those same six questions apply to your business? Let's see.

1. Who are your ideal prospects?

   Companies that purchase large machines that do what your machines do.

2. What is it that sets them apart and makes them identifiable among the general population?

   They are in the business of making large channels out of flat pieces of steel.

3. How can you reach them?

   They read industry trade journals, belong to the Association of Steel Benders, they display at industry trade shows, they attend industry trade shows.

4. What problems do they have that you can solve?

   The machine they are currently using takes one of about every eight pieces of steel they stick into it and twists it into the shape of a pretzel!

5. What keeps them up at night?

   Unhappy customers because of missed deadlines, unhappy customers because of poor quality channels, a huge pile of pretzel-shaped pieces of steel out behind the shop.

6. What is the most effective way to reach them?

   Advertise in industry trade journals, send them direct mail letters, rent space at a tradeshow, team up with other vendors they do business with.

So your business is not different. You've identified who you want to do business with and why. You know who your prospective customers are and how to reach them. You know what problems they have and how you can solve their problems.

You have joined the conversation they are having with themselves.

Now, using the effective advertising copywriting techniques that you've learned here, put together a sales letter and start mailing to them over and over.

Send them a letter, then craft a second letter that is very similar to and references the first letter you sent them. Then a third, a fourth, a fifth and a sixth.

Don't be cheap and stupid. You are asking them to give you thousands, tens of thousands, probably even hundreds of thousands of dollars. Spend some money to attract the attention of this valuable customer. Send them FedEx packages. Send them anything you can think of that will get their attention and make them read your sales letter.

I know of a very successful direct mailer who sends the same prospective customers fourteen different packages in the mail before he gives up on them. And the product he is selling only has a price tag of around $1,000. But he does the math on each mailing he does, and he knows that it's profitable to mail to them fourteen times. In many cases it's only after the fourteenth attempt that they finally decide to do business with him.

Don't be cheap or lazy.

Delegate it and be firm. Make sure these mailings or contacts go out as scheduled. Make sure nothing interrupts the process once it is set into motion.

Set up the contact and follow-up system, and make sure it is working. Then delegate someone in your organization to identify prospective customers and get them into the system. Run it on a till forbid basis.

It will be "vending machine predictable".

Remember the analogy. Drop in a coin, turn the crank, out comes the money. Drop in another coin, out comes more money. Now all you have to do is put it on autopilot.

I'm Melting, I'm Melting!

Remember that line from *The Wizard of Oz*?

As I write this and as you read it, there are small businesses all over the country that are melting. They used to be *this big*, now they are only *this big* and shrinking by the day.

It's not their fault. Between government regulations and intervention and all of those big box stores, they are being pushed out of business.

That's a bunch of crap!

I'm sorry to be so blunt, but it's true. Being successful in business means that you watch the market and adapt as it changes. Sure, things are different. Things are always going to be different. Things are always changing.

The smart entrepreneur invests in themselves, constantly reading books, investing in programs that will help them grow their business, and participating in at least one mastermind group to help them brainstorm for new ideas on how to grow their business.

In my town we have a small printshop that I've done business with for years. These days I buy less printing than I have in years past, so I don't get in there very often. But each time I go in, it depresses me to see how little they have going on.

Why is that? Why do they have so little going on?

Because the owner does little, if anything at all, to stimulate new business or to stimulate business from past customers. The business is shrinking. And like all shrinking businesses, eventually the business shrinks to the point that it becomes necessary to close the doors just to stop the bleeding of cash flow in the wrong direction.

No matter what business you are in, you lose customers by the day. In some cases you might have done something wrong, but no matter how good you are, people move away, die, or go out of business. You must have a "vending machine predictable" method of marketing working for you constantly to bring new customers into your business.

So how do you fix the little printshop? How do you reverse this situation?

With this particular business, my solution would be simple.

First of all, you cannot do business with people who don't even know that you exist. You have to raise your hand and say, "Hey, here I am! I really would like to do business with you."

Keep in mind, this is a small printshop that caters to small businesses, salespeople, and individuals who need printing for personal, charitable, or civic events. They are really not positioned to take on large print jobs for really big customers. Not that they couldn't, but that's not their primary goal for a lot of different reasons. At least not at the moment.

So specific to this print shop and their ideal prospect, this is what I'd test first. I'd start running small newspaper ads with an offer like this:

Business Card Special!
500 Business Cards only $4.97
This price includes Design,
Printing and FREE delivery.
Call Right Now!
000-000-0000
Fax your card layout to:
000-000-0000

Now keep in mind, sure, this is a crazy low-price offer that you cannot possibly profit from. At least not on the first transaction. But there are a few things to consider:

1. This printshop has very little work. So instead of standing around with nothing to do, they might as well be printing some inexpensive business cards.

2. Anybody who needs a business card is at least a reasonable prospect for additional printing. They

may need flyers, letterheads, stationery, printed envelopes, catalogs, price lists, postcards, color postcards, better-quality business cards or photo business cards.

3. Free delivery. As a salesperson, what is the most difficult part of your job? Getting an appointment with a prospective buyer. If you call me and ask for an appointment to stop by, I know you are going to try to sell me and I really don't have the time, or I'm just not interested.

But if you call me and want to deliver the business cards I ordered from you, what can I say? Of course I'm going to give you a time to deliver the cards. After all, I ordered them and I have yet to pay you. I have an obligation to meet with you. And since the appointment is to take delivery, I don't even suspect that you are going to try to sell me.

And you are not going to try to sell me. But we are going to have a brief conversation and I will get to meet you, maybe learn a little about you, and you will give me several samples of the many things you can print for me. And if you're smart, the price for each item will be printed right on the item with an easy way for me to order that particular item if I am interested.

And before you leave, you will suggest how I might be able to use those items to grow my own business.

End of transaction.

I am no longer a stranger and no longer a prospective customer. I am now your customer. You should add me to your customer mailing list and mail to me once a month. You should be sending me a newsletter once a month that tells me how to grow my business using your products. More about that later.

Remember what you read earlier? *Run it on a till forbid basis!*

I can assure you, if my printshop owner in this example would run the advertisement that I just showed you, and follow up with delivery as I described, this advertising campaign would be so successful that he or she could run it forever, or until they just couldn't handle any more new business.

It would be "vending machine predictable". Drop in the money, turn the crank, and out comes a steady stream of new business.

There is an old saying among people in the field of sales that goes something like this: "To be successful in sales all you have to do is see more people, belly to belly, every day."

And it's true. And of course if you prequalify the people who you see belly to belly, the number of people you convert into customers will be higher. A lot higher.

So that's what the small, unassuming newspaper advertisement in this example does for the printshop owner. It sets up the belly-to-belly meeting with a qualified prospect. And it does it in such a way that the printshop owner is welcomed in with open arms. It's very different from cold calling on someone who just doesn't want you bothering them.

When you meet this customer belly to belly, you learn things about them and their business, then you can tailor future marketing efforts around what you know about them.

Think about your business. Can you do something similar in your business? What small marketing tool can you put into action on a till forbid basis that will be "vending machine predictable"?

Now's let's change directions.

Oh No, Walmart is Coming to Town

Now what are we going to do?

Panic? That's what most small businesses do when a big chain store decides to move into their town. Or they just give up, roll over and die.

Here's something to think about . . .

There are hundreds, if not thousands of small towns around the country that don't have a Walmart or any other big box store and probably never will. Why do you suppose that is?

It's because there just aren't enough people, or not enough income in that particular market area to support a big box store. Which also means that there is a limited amount of money to be traded each day.

Which would you rather have? A market that has no money to spend, or a market that is lucrative enough to support Walmart and a few other big box stores?

I hope you see the advantage of being in a market that is so lucrative that it can support multiple big box stores. That means there are tens of thousands of dollars being traded each day, and your job is to come in under the radar and grab *more than your fair share* of that money.

Did you catch that? I said "more than your fair share".

This isn't preschool where the cookies and milk gets divided up evenly. This is the business world where those who are smart enough to invest in programs like this and learn how to out-market their competitors are entitled to grab all the business they can.

Or better yet, grab the best customers, the best clients, those who are willing to pay premium prices for high quality goods and services and leave what you don't want for your competitors to fight over. Let them have the scraps! They'd do it to you in a heartbeat if they knew how.

So from now on, when you drive by Walmart and any other big box store, I want you to smile and think how lucky you are and realize how easy they are to compete with. I'll give you a perfect example.

Just yesterday I went to a big box home store to get a rather unique lightbulb. While there, my wife and I went down to the garden area to see if they had any roses. I found a display of roses but many of them looked kind of sad. I asked the guy working in the garden area if they had any other roses, and he pointed to a rack behind me and said, "Right there, I think those are roses." This poor guy didn't know a rose from a juniper, yet they had him working in the garden section!

144

People hate that!

They want somebody to lead them to the roses, point out which ones are the hardiest in their climate zone, give them some planting and care tips, and tell them how to get the plants to produce beautiful flowers all summer long.

People love that and they will honor you with more and more patronage if you do that for them.

No matter what you sell!

Had I been at a full-service garden center, that probably would have happened. But first of all, I need a reason to go to that full-service garden center. Give me a reason to come by and meet you! And give it to me often so I don't forget about you.

That's what "Turn the Crank Marketing" is about. Bringing in a steady stream of new customers, giving them plenty of good reasons to come back, then staying in touch with them so they don't forget about you.

The Rule of 250 and Staying in Touch

What is the absolutely worst thing that almost all
small businesses in America do that is costing them
thousands of dollars each month?

They fail to stay in touch with their customers.

Most business owners spend all their time and resources
looking for (or hoping for) new customers. New
customers are great, but not if you are only going to
neglect them and make them ex-customers.

People are busy. Really busy. And they honestly
do forget about you, then the next time they need
something they just go somewhere else. Your
customers should be addicted to you, and I'll show you
a really easy way to make that happen.

The very first thing you should be doing is collecting
the names and addresses of all your customers. A few
business owners do this, but not most. And very few use
those names and addresses as they should. The easiest
way to do that is to run some kind of a contest and give

away a prize that your customers would really like to have. This is a really inexpensive way to capture those names and addresses. Make sure the prize you offer is of true value, and not some piece of junk you've got laying around the shop.

Then you should enter those names and addresses into a database. A simple Excel spreadsheet will work just fine. Keep in mind, you are going to mail to this list often, and as your mailing list grows you'll eventually want to turn over the job of mailing the list to a professional mail shop. So make sure the database you use can also be used by a mail shop. Pick up the phone and call a couple mail shops to ask them what software they can work with and what they cannot. Think ahead. You'll find mail shops in the yellow pages.

Now this is where you are going to get really cheap on me and refuse to do this. Please don't do that!

If you really and truly want to build your business, you will mail to your entire mailing list a minimum of once a month. The easiest way to do this is to send out a newsletter about you and your business each month.

It doesn't have to be fancy, and it doesn't have to be ten pages. It should be about four pages. Also include a different promotion each month. Maybe a percentage off sale "this week only". Maybe a gift certificate they can give to a friend. Something of value. Not something you think has value. *Something your customers will consider valuable!*

Writing a newsletter once a month sounds easy enough, but for most people it's not that easy and they don't make the time to get it done. They procrastinate about doing it, then next thing you know they lose interest after mailing only a few issues because they decide it's not working.

Don't be foolish!

This works, and it works better than you can imagine. But you have to be consistent and just keep mailing it with almost blind faith. Month after month just mail the newsletter and make a special offer each and every month.

Think about it. Think this through. In this book you have discovered dozens of things that you probably did not know before about your business, about your customers, about people in general. If you apply what you've learned here to your newsletter and the special offer you make each and every month, how can it not work to help build your business?

Coming up with content for your newsletter is pretty easy if you just keep a notepad nearby, and as customers ask you questions, jot them down. Each of those questions could probably be a topic for your newsletter. But your newsletter should not be all about your business.

You can include a few lines each month about yourself. People love to know what you've been up to, what you do in your spare time, how many kids or grandkids you have, etc. Don't bore them to death, just give them a little peek inside your life each month. That will make your newsletter addicting, and it will permanently embed you and your business into the minds of your customers so they cannot forget about you.

You should also include other tidbits that are completely unrelated to your business. Maybe a few lines of inspiration each month. A quote or two. People love to read that stuff, but they like it in small doses. So if they know you'll give them a small dose each month, they'll look forward to reading your newsletter.

Listen to me!!!

If you do this, if you publish a small four-page newsletter each and every month, your customers will be so addicted to it that, if you were to skip a month, they'll call you up and ask about it. They will think about you and your business *ten times more often* because of your newsletter.

Remember the Rule of 250. Each person you do business with, on average, knows 250 people. They will talk about you and your business to those 250 people. A few of them will become your customers because of your newsletter and your special offers, and they also know 250 people.

Growing a business is as simple as *exploiting the Rule of 250!*

Now these are the questions that you are going to ask:

"Can't I just email it?"

No, absolutely not. Email is a wonderful tool to be used for the right things at the right time, but it's all wrong for this type of newsletter. People are deluged with email and spam and they will not be happy with you emailing them without their explicit permission.

But even if you have their permission to email them, you still need to mail this newsletter the old-fashioned way for it to work as intended. This is a stand-alone marketing tool that can and will build your business if you simply allow it to.

Here's your next question to me:

"Do I have to mail it every month? Can't I just mail it quarterly or every other month?"

No. Don't be cheap or lazy. It will only cost you sixty or seventy cents to mail these newsletters, if that. That's $8.40 per year, per customer. What is the lifetime value of your average customer?

This works.

A carpet cleaner who was barely squeaking out a living went from barely getting by to a very attractive six figure income by doing only four things differently in his business.

1. He started mailing a newsletter to his existing customers monthly. Never missed an issue.

2. Two weeks after each newsletter, he mailed them a postcard restating the special offer he made in the newsletter.

3. On a regular basis, he mailed a simple direct-mail sales letter to upscale homes. Instead of competing in the low end of the market where he had been like all other carpet cleaners, he decided *who he wanted to do business with* and marketed exclusively to upscale homes.

Remember how I suggested that the auto repair shop owner should target people with higher incomes in his market area and mail over and over to them with the free oil change offer?

When the carpet cleaner mailed to the upscale homes, he sent them a $25 gift certificate and a letter that explained how he was different from the other cleaners in the area. It worked incredibly well.

He sent them a *gift certificate*, not a coupon. There is a huge difference in the mind of the person receiving it. People get coupons day in and day out, but how often does someone take the time to send them an actual gift certificate?

What's the difference? A gift certificate is printed on heavier paper with a textured surface, it has a certificate border, and it should be hand signed, or at least appear to be hand signed in blue ink. It also comes in its own little envelope that is placed inside the letter. The envelope should also indicate on the outside that it contains a gift certificate.

People throw away coupons by the dozen, but nobody throws away a gift certificate.

It's all about perception.

4. He raised his prices. Because the first three techniques were working so well and he had so much more business, it only made sense to raise his prices and he started marketing more and more to those who would pay his higher price. This one simple technique works better than you can imagine.

Four simple steps and he more than tripled his net income.

This stuff works!

Remember the printshop example I showed you earlier? I suggested that once the printshop lands a new customer with the low-priced business card offer, they should start mailing that customer a newsletter every month with a special offer. What the carpet cleaner did would work perfectly for the printshop. Mail a newsletter with a special offer, let's say 500 printed envelopes for $30. Two weeks after the newsletter is mailed, send out a postcard stating that the special envelope price is only good for seven more days.

In the newsletter, the printshop owner could also suggest promotional ideas for his customers that would help them grow their businesses. Promotional ideas that would require printed materials or advertising specialties.

It's all about sparking ideas.

If there's one thing that will stop you from mailing this newsletter monthly, it will be finding the time to get it written. It's not that difficult for some people, but extremely difficult for others. And for that I have a solution.

We create a generic, but very interesting monthly newsletter for businesses just like yours. About eighty percent of the newsletter is done for you. All you have to do is fill in a few lines specific to your business.

You can get samples of our "almost ready to mail newsletters" at **http://TurntheCrankMarketing.com** so you can at least get an idea of what your newsletter should look like.

If You Owned the Local Newspaper and Could Advertise for Free, How Often Would You Advertise?

Every day, right?

Our local newspaper serves most of three counties and has a circulation of about 65,000 last time I checked their numbers. I've advertised in this paper many times with incredible results. I almost always get a return of twenty to one or better on the money I've invested in the ads that I've run.

Then a few years back I discovered the internet and national and sometimes even global marketing, and I started building my own email mailing list. A list of people who have given me permission to mail them any time I want. The way they give me permission to mail to them is they add themselves to my mailing list. I never add people to my mailing list, even if they ask me to.

If they ask me to add them to my mailing list I send them to the online form so they can add themselves to the list. This is important because when they add themselves to the list, the list service that I use logs their

IP address so I can easily prove that I did not mail to them without their permission. That's really important with email marketing.

For a number of years now I have been building a mailing list, and over the years I made a lot of mistakes, used the wrong software, then I used the wrong list service and on and on. I've quite literally thrown away tens of thousands of subscribers because I screwed up.

But despite the many mistakes that I've made, I now have a list of 137,000 subscribers who have given me permission to send them emails. That's more than double the subscriber base of our local newspaper.

That's 137,000 people that I can market to for free!

Every Monday evening I sit down and send a message to my mailing list. I keep the message short and I make it useful and interesting so they stay on my list. I mail to them on Monday evening, and almost immediately the money starts coming in. We spend the next seven days processing the orders, sending out the products, and banking the money. Then I do it again the following Monday evening.

Just one email a week typically brings in between $4,500 and $8,000, and occasionally $10,000 or more. And as I write this book, I am simultaneously implementing strategies that should double those numbers. I am implementing the very same strategies in my own business that I am teaching you here.

Not in a million years did I ever think that making money could be this easy!

My friend, the internet is here to stay. It's constantly changing, but it's not going away. Don't ignore it. Learn to harness it, no matter what you sell. On my **TurntheCrankMarketing.com** website I have a free report about how I build and maintain my mailing list. There are days when we will easily add 350 new subscribers or more in one day to the mailing list! Discover how I do it. Get the report.

Do More for Your Customers; Reward Them!

This is something that most of us are terrible at, me included. When people give you money, you should say 'thank you' and all of that. But you should probably do more.

Years ago I did business with a guy who admittedly only made it through the eighth grade, and I suspect he struggled to get that far. Everybody called him Big Mel because he was a huge man. Probably 450 pounds. Doing business with him was always interesting to say the least, but I did a lot of business with him, and at times he and I would bicker for ten minutes over ten dollars. Not because either of us cared about the ten dollars at stake, but because neither of us wanted to be wrong. But we never got mad at each other, we just bickered.

But Big Mel did something for me that nobody else I had done business with had ever done, and he did it many times over the years. We were both in seasonal businesses and when it was busy, it was busy! But when things slowed down I'd often pop in just to say 'hi' and exchange some wisdom.

But two or three times a year, Mel would say, "I feel like giving something away, Maaiiike," in his southern drawl. "Go over there and pick yourself out a shovel off that rack. Any shovel, just take one." Mel did this because I was one of his best customers, and he wanted me to know that he appreciated my business. I wonder how many others got shovels? I know my kids got hats, gloves, pens, you name it, each time they rode with me.

Big Mel wasn't the only person I was doing business with at the time. There were nurseries that I was spending thousands of dollars a week with, and not one of them ever showed me that kind of appreciation.

Big Mel is no longer with us. He died way too young. I don't know if it was the kindness or the obesity, but his big heart just gave out one day.

When you have good loyal customers, I want you to think about Big Mel, and let them know that you appreciate their business.

Go Find Those Ex-Customers of Yours and Give Them a Good Reason to Come Back

We all have ex-customers, and most of us make the mistake of thinking that they don't want to do business with us any more or they'd be doing business with us today.

That's wrong. There's a reason why they are not doing business with you today. They left for a reason. Some die, some move away, but the rest can and should be lured back. You lost them to your competition either because you may have somehow alienated them, or maybe you just neglected them.

Remember Big Mel? People want to feel appreciated. Dig out all of those old addresses and send them a letter. Let them know that you miss them and that you are sorry if you somehow let them down. Then give them a gift certificate. Go back and review what I wrote about the gift certificate the carpet cleaner used.

Think about this.

How many businesses are there that you used to do business with but don't now, or haven't in a long time? Have any of them ever made an attempt to find out why you left? Have any of them ever sent you a gift certificate to get you to come back?

Had they made the effort, you'd probably be doing business with them today.

Never forget about the *lifetime value of a customer* and the *Rule of 250*. The Rule of 250 can work for you or against you, and only you can decide whose team you want those ex-customers rooting for.

Business to Business Marketing

This is where I am supposed to give you the *silver bullet of marketing to businesses.* But the truth is, there is no such silver bullet. Marketing to businesses is done the exact same way that you market to consumers.

Ask yourself these six questions:

1. Who are your ideal prospects?

2. What is it that sets them apart and makes them identifiable among the general population?

3. How can you reach them?

4. What problems do they have that you can solve?

5. What keeps them up at night?

6. What is the most effective way to reach them?

Then you apply everything that you have learned in this book. Psychology still applies because businesses don't make buying decisions, people do. Real live people with the same emotions that you and I have.

Think about that. Giving consideration to the emotions of your business-to-business buyers can give you a huge advantage over your competitors because nobody else gives this an ounce of thought. All they think about is how bad they'd like to sell to a certain business. When in fact, they should be considering what is really going to drive the buying decision.

Remember when I showed you that list of emotional triggers earlier? They still apply, maybe even more so in business-to-business selling. People at work have an entirely different set of emotions to deal with, but they are there, and they are very real, and they are on the list I showed you.

With business-to-business marketing, direct mail is often the very best way to reach your prospective customers. Use the copywriting skills that you've learned here. Put great care into how you craft the direct-mail letters, postcards, and any other advertising pieces that you might use to get the attention of the business prospects you are trying to reach.

Don't be cheap!

How many times have I said that? Business to business usually means a significant amount of money, and over time, a great deal of income for you and your business. Contact them over and over. Send them a sequence of letters that push all the buttons, all the emotional triggers you can think of, and just keep coming back to them over and over.

Remember the example I gave you of the guy who mails business owners fourteen different times before he gives up on them? And his product only sells for about $1,000. You can afford to go at them many, many times.

The Anatomy of a Sales Letter

A sales letter is nothing more than an advertisement disguised as a letter. It should look like a letter and be personal in nature, but it should contain all of the powerful elements of a good advertisement.

A sales letter can have a bold headline like I've used many times throughout this publication. Or you can instead use the opening sentence as your headline. I've done both with great results, and since you are going to create a series of these letters, change it up and see if you can determine which works better for you.

What's really important is to keep in mind that the opening sentence is the headline, and you should put as much time and effort into the opening sentence as you would when searching for a powerful headline. It's that important.

When writing headlines, you should sit down with a stack of 3" by 5" index cards and just start brainstorming for powerful headlines. Write as many as you can, one per card, then review them, and as you do, brainstorm for more and write them down. You should try to write out at least one hundred headlines as you search for *the perfect headline*.

You should also put the same amount of effort into finding the perfect opening sentence for your sales letter. Something that will grab the prospects' attention and pull them into the rest of the letter.

The body of the letter should follow the same pattern as a good advertisement. Get their attention, arouse their interest, build their desire and then ask them to take action. Tell them exactly what you want them to do. Tell them exactly how they should respond.

Also in the letter, figure out what objections they might have, just as they would if you were standing in front of their desk trying to sell them, and dispel those objections right then and there in the letter.

After you ask for the order, close the letter with a businesslike salutation, and sign each letter by hand, or have the signature printed in blue ink to look as if you actually hand signed it.

For effect, you can also handwrite a few notes in the margin of the letter, or circle a really important phrase that you want to make sure they read. I know this sounds unprofessional, but it's not about looking professional. It's about getting their attention and acquiring them as a customer.

Your letter must contain a PS. The postscript is actually one of the most read parts of a letter. People open a letter, they really don't want to read it so they are looking for a good reason not to read it, so they flip to the last page, see who signed it, and read the PS.

The postscript needs to be as powerful as the opening sentence or headline. The postscript should grab their attention and make them *want to read your letter!* Spend a great deal of time on the postscript.

The envelope!

The envelope that you mail the letter in is more important than the letter, because if the envelope doesn't get opened, all of your opportunities with the prospect are out the window.

There are two schools of thought about envelopes, and they are both correct. You have to see what works best for you.

The first school of thought, and the least popular, but maybe the most effective and the safest bet, is to send your letter in a plain white envelope with just a return address. No business name, no teaser copy on the envelope, and no printed address label. And you must use a real live stamp, not a bulk mail indicium.

The second school of thought is to put some teaser copy on the envelope, or lots of teaser copy on the envelope. It just depends on who you are mailing to, and what you are trying to sell them.

The idea behind the plain white envelope, and it has been proven over and over, is that curiosity alone will get the envelope opened. Which is really important since hundreds of thousands of direct-mail letters a day get thrown out unopened in this country alone.

So when sending the plain white envelope, your prospect is not likely to throw it away because he or she has no idea what's in it. So it goes into the "A pile" that needs to be opened soon.

But let's say that you sell diecast models of NASCAR cars, and you have a list of people who are NASCAR junkies. They buy anything and everything NASCAR. Which is better? A plain white envelope, or an envelope that clearly indicates that it contains "*a time sensitive offer from NASCAR*". The envelope that contains all of the NASCAR teaser copy probably would do the trick because it might get opened faster than the bills and letters from the IRS.

How do you know which to use? You have to test. Send out two thousand letters. A thousand in one envelope, a thousand in the other, then measure the results. But . . . when doing a test like this everything else has to be identical so you know for sure that it was the envelope that made the difference. And I do mean *everything else has to be identical.*

Here are a few more twists that will get your envelope opened and probably get your letter read. On the outside of the envelope print the words, as if they were stamped onto the envelope with a rubber stamp, "Do Not Bend Photograph Enclosed". Then include an interesting and intriguing snapshot that will make the prospect think. Keep in mind that the job of the snapshot is to draw the prospect into the sales letter.

Another little twist that will get your envelope opened is to use the plain white envelope, and instead of printing a return address on the envelope, use those cute little return address labels that come on a roll. You know, like the ones that your Aunt Mary uses. Trust me, your envelope will get opened.

Come Off as a Real Person . . .

I'm going to leave you with a little advertising copywriting tip I hope you grasp, because it will give your marketing teeth!

Each and every time you sit down to create an advertisement of any kind, I want you to refer to this manual and follow the outline that I've established for you. Use the psychological triggers that I've taught you. But also write as if you are writing to your old friend from high school. Don't make it businesslike. Make it friendly and fun to read.

And with that said, here are some down-to-earth phrases that you can use . . .

Yeah right . . . like we'd fall for that
Give us a jingle-jangle right now
Magical powers
Like some kind of a cheap date
Swore under oath
He babbled about this or that
Super duper

Real McCoy
Don't let anyone in your family suffer
Gotta run . . .
This will rock your business! (with rock attached)
Squatter's rights
Contractor-infested
Someone who just might have the same last name
    as me
Fatal flaw
Social proof
Those folks out in the "burbs"
Market share cannibalism
Renegade group of
Double whammy
Big, fast and easy
I thought it had to be that way
Money coming in day and night
Worked very, very hard, still had no money, time or
    freedom
Trading time for money is dumb
Ditch-digger hard work

Be on the lookout for more phrases like this and add to this list regularly.

Okay, that's it!

Now get you butt on over to **TurntheCrankMarketing. com** and locate a **Mastermind Group** in your area. There's a lot of other really cool stuff there as well, including more hot ideas to make you more money!

Stop waiting for somebody to come along and give you permission to succeed. It's not going to happen. It's on you. You have to anoint yourself "Marketing Expert" of your business and then start applying your expertise to your business, and keep implementing new ideas.

Then you have to anoint yourself "Personal Success Coach" and find more ways, maybe outside of your current business, to take your success to the next level.

It's possible that you could find that next level at **TurntheCrankMarketing.com.** Check it out.

As always, stay inspired!

Yours in incredible success,

Michael J. McGroarty

LaVergne, TN USA
30 September 2009
159396LV00004B/3/P